LAST TRAIN
TO ELKMONT

A look back
at life on Little River
in the Great Smoky Mountains

By VIC WEALS

Published by

OLDEN PRESS

Post Office Box 14
Kodak, TN 37764
vic.weals@gmail.com

Softcover Edition

ISBN 0-9629156-1-0

Graphic Design and Production
The TypeCase, Knoxville, TN 37919

Printed at

Quad/Graphics, Fairfield, Pennsylvania 2011

Cover Photo: As a "postcard engine," one of the functions of Little River's No. 105 was to pose for advertising of passenger excursions to the summer resort at Elkmont. Scene of the photograph made about 1910 was under Indian Head Rock in Little River Gorge. The Baldwin 2-6-2 was also a work engine and was the final locomotive to make a run all the way to Elkmont, to begin taking up the rails from that end late in 1925. The story of the sudden dismantling of the Elkmont line, and the building of an automobile road to replace it, begins on Page 85.

The forests of old in the Great Smoky Mountains

Excerpt from a paper by George B. Sudworth as read before a meeting of the American Forestry Association in Nashville on Sept. 23, 1897.

"The broad mountain slopes and deep, gorgelike coves lower down have a forest cover of truly virgin character. In some of the eastern border counties, where railways have yet to come, the silence of those somber forest depths is scarcely ever broken by the sound of the woodman's ax. Primeval forests of centuries guard the cold crystal streams that flow on throughout the year. Bear and deer slake their thirst from the clear bubbling pools of these streams and somewhere in their hidden, winding courses the moonshiner brings life into the "mountain dew." Huge tulip trees (poplars), with ages numbered in centuries, crowd the deep coves and rich mountainsides with their gigantic forms.

"The sugar maple, which we expect to find in perfection only in a northern forest, is represented here in great numbers and in the finest development. So, too, is the familiar beech. The little-known yellow buckeye is nowhere else surpassed in its great height and diameter growth. The cucumber magnolia, a rival of the tulip tree in the appearance and excellence of its timber, occurs plentifully and of large size in these forests, together with the much-valued white ash, three to five feet in diameter and with 60 feet of clear trunk.

"Here too the southern white-leaved basswood grows to fine dimensions, scattered in small and large groups throughout the region. The abundance of big chestnut timber in this region makes the large chestnut of the coast region look small."

Foreword

The Hotel Elkmont was seldom confused with the Wonderland Hotel or the Appalachian Club, the latter two being much more elegant.

The Hotel Elkmont was more often called "the boardinghouse." It was a rough board shack covered with tarpaper on its weather sides. There were beds, mostly for workers who didn't have their families at Elkmont. Each boarder sat in an assigned place at mealtime, and newcomers stood until the regulars were seated.

There were wash basins on a stand outside the door, and a water bucket from which the basins could be refilled. A fresh towel made of a flour sack was hung nearby for each meal, one towel for the use of everybody. Homemade lye soap for lathering was the *soap du jour.*

Pauline Parton was 12 years old when she first worked at the posher Wonderland Hotel, cleaning rooms. That was in 1929, four years after the last train had run and the railroad been dismantled, the boardinghouse closed and the loggers departed. Elkmont was now a quieter resort reachable only by automobile.

The next summer Pauline worked in the hotel pantry, making salads, cutting pies, slicing bread. Frank and Bea Smith did the cooking and baked the bread and pastries. The Smiths were kind to Pauline, a favorable start to her life career of managing and owning restaurants. In 1993, Pauline Parton Talbot Hughes was retired and remembering Elkmont nostalgically. The Wonderland Hotel, her first place to work for pay, had closed forever at the end of 1992, 80 years after it was built.

Homer Bales was 94 years old and back in Gatlinburg in May of 1993, staying a spell at a motel he and his family had built years earlier, at the end of a logging career that began when he was 13 years old. Homer worked at logging on upper Little River before World War I, before he was 18 years old. He worked at A.J. Huff's Gatlinburg sawmill on Baskins Creek well before that, starting when he was 13 years old, taking boards from the steam-powered circular saw and standing them on end to air-dry. Output was about 10,000 board feet of lumber per 10-hour work day, and Homer's clothes soon would be dripping sweat. He worked awhile at Crestmont on Big Creek, on the North Carolina side of the Smokies. But he asked to be excused from reciting the details of all that. Since the death of wife Pearl five years earlier, it was painful for him to try to recall specifics of the past. Pearl made life easier by doing a lot of remembering for him.

Eldridge Ownby, 91 years old in 1993 and living at Mark Hill Manor in Sevierville, told of his childhood on Jakes Creek above Elkmont, one of seven children of Newt and Polly Ownby. He was nearly six years old when the railroad came to Elkmont late in 1908. Before the rails were taken up 17 years later, he was working for the Little River Lumber Co. in the logging of Jakes Creek. It was the last area cut in the upper valley of East Prong of Little River, of which Elkmont was the hub. "It was an exciting place, with trains coming and going. There's never been anything like it since," Eldridge said.

The brothers John, Baus, Odie, and Eldridge Ownby moved to Tremont after 1925, and stayed until that valley was logged out in the late 1930s, and the land turned over to Great Smoky Mountains National Park. The brothers rode the last trainload of logs to the Townsend mill in 1938. "John was the main one," Eldridge would recall when he was the only brother left. "John had the contract with the lumber company, but we worked at it together. We logged in places where the overhead skidders couldn't reach. We brought the timber to the railroad with horse teams."

Baus and Odie drove teams. John ran the blacksmith shop, which was moved often and at times truly was "beneath the spreading chestnut tree." John kept the horses shod, made tools. Eldridge cut timber, sharpened saws, drove a team some. Their older half-brother Otha worked with them several years. Life was orderly in the Ownby camp—the work day 10 hours, six days a week. Their wives and children were in camp with them at least part of the time, living in the little boxcar-shaped houses set off from flatcars with a log crane. All five brothers were able to buy farms in Sevier County when the job ended.

Florence Cope Bush gave information and pictures for the chapter, "Light at the End of Logging," which begins on Page 89 and is the story of her family. Flo's own biography of her mother, "Dorie—Woman of the Mountains," is published by University of Tennessee Press.

"Last Train to Elkmont" does not pretend to be an objective history of the lumber industry on Little River. It is offered instead to help preserve the memory of resourceful people who lived and worked there early in the 20th Century, before the creation of Great Smoky Mountains National Park. A final incentive to publish the book was new information on the life of William Marion Walker from his last surviving children. Walker was the hunter and wilderness keeper who tried to save the great trees of Thunderhead Prong, and succeeded up to his own death.

For most of the book we owe the families who shared their memories and old pictures. For answers to last-minute questions, we turned to the few loggers or their wives surviving in the 'Nineties, and more often found only the children left. This foreword is being written last, its purpose to acknowledge the help of several not mentioned elsewhere in the book.

—Vic Weals

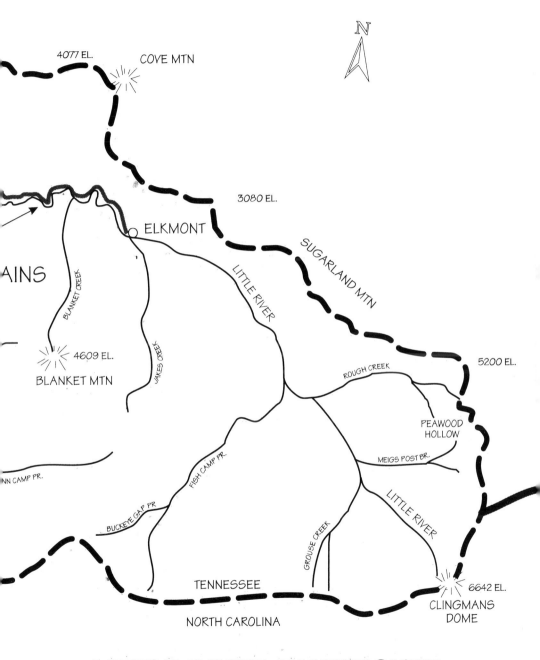

4077 EL.   COVE MTN

N

3080 EL.

ELKMONT

SUGARLAND MTN

LITTLE RIVER

AINS

BLANKET CREEK

4609 EL.

BLANKET MTN

JAKES CREEK

ROUGH CREEK

5200 EL.

PEAWOOD
HOLLOW

MEIGS POST BR.

NN CAMP PR.

FISH CAMP PR.

LITTLE RIVER

BUCKEYE GAP PR.

GROUSE CREEK

TENNESSEE

6642 EL.

CLINGMANS
DOME

NORTH CAROLINA

LITTLE RIVER WATERSHED

Scale 2   **0**   **2**   **4 Miles**

Knoxville, Tenn.
December, 1990

Ten years ago a Knoxville Journal editorial foretold in modest terms the future historical value of the perceptive reporting of the past by Vic Weals in his Tennessee Travels column. Today this present volume serves to confirm that judgment.

In this book Vic Weals is himself composing history in a certain sense. He revitalizes times gone by, but he does so still as the observant reporter, not as an erudite historian who has a thesis, evaluates critically, makes opinionated surmises and moralizes. Weals leaves it to the readers to form their own opinions.

The many photographs in these pages complement the word pictures transmitted by Weals, characterizing the singular Little River people with their individual ways, their hardihood and their originative exploits.

Dudley Brewer
retired columnist
and editorial writer,
The Knoxville Journal

Contents

1

In the beginning there was Eden's Garden

The Little River logging frenzy started in the last years of the 19th Century, before the railroad came. It began with the cutting of the giant yellow poplars, some nearly eight feet in diameter, in the flats of lower East Prong and Middle Prong upstream from Tuckaleechee Cove.

The band mill that could saw logs of such a size was more than 20 miles downriver, below Rockford at Roddy Branch. The old highway between Knoxville and Maryville passes the site.

Splash dam with Will Walker standing on it is believed to be one built by the English Lumber Co. on Middle Fork of Little River above the mouth of Spruce Flats Branch, on or near Walker's property. There was a way to open the center gate fully and suddenly, to release a head of water to float logs to a sawmill more than 20 miles down Little River. Photo made from the downstream side.

The logs were rolled to the riverbed close to where they were cut, to be moved downstream to the sawmill on surges of water turned loose from man-made splash dams. There were two such dams on the East Prong and two on Middle Prong.

A poplar log was cut about a foot longer to insure that it would arrive at the sawmill 16 feet long, because it would be damaged at both ends while it bumped and bruised down the rocky gorges.

Roy Mack Myers (right) and friend Oscar Tipton as young men in Tuckaleechee Cove early in the 20th Century. Their black felt hats served as a kind of safety helmet, to protect the head somewhat in fights, falls, and brushes with low tree branches.

The logging operation and possibly the Rockford sawmill with it was an enterprise headed by John L. English, who appears to have risen quickly as a Knoxville lawyer and as a businessman.

Roy M. Myers was born in Tuckaleechee Cove in 1889 in a home a few yards above Little River. In interviews more than 80 years later, he recalled the English company's log drives of his childhood. He had stood on the bank and seen them race by on the flood, and had them further impressed on his memory by the reminiscence of older neighbors through the years.

Grant Miller moved to Blount County in the 1890s to be foreman of river drives for English, and it was Miller's delight in later years to find people with whom he could share his memories. Because he came often to the home of Roy and Florence Myers, and because their son Harry listened with interest, we know something today of how Miller did his job.

When conditions could be controlled, river drives began in the morning. Men wearing calked boots rode the big logs by stepping or leaping from one to another. They carried pike poles for balance, or to free logs caught in brush or in eddies. The first crew of drivers would ride about 10 miles, a distance that gave them time to walk back to their homes upriver before dark. A second crew herded the logs the remaining distance to Roddy Branch.

The drivers stayed with the main body of logs, ignoring the occasional strays stranded in eddies, Miller said. They pulled the strays back to the current in a second sweep, and moved them downriver on new floods from the splash dams.

Roy Myers remembered the winter of early 1899 when English had hundreds of logs waiting on the banks, each of them branded with the company's "E." The timber-cutters of that busy season included the brothers Len and Ave Cogdill, both about six feet, six inches tall and axmen of exceptional skill.

River drives could be made more safely on a swollen stream, if they could be combined with the timely release of water from the dams. But rain and melting snow produced a flood one evening that was enough to float every log in its reach, without the help of drivers or of splash dams. It was the Little River flood of Feb. 6, 1899, and it washed away one of the dams on East Prong above Tuckaleechee Cove.

Sherman Myers and his two oldest sons, Wade and Roy, stood in awe in the dark as the logs "came jamming bump! bump! bump!, the river full of them," in Roy's words. There was ice along the banks, and a log "as thick as a king-size mattress is wide" somehow slid across it to the road near them.

"Let's go to the house," Sherman said suddenly to his boys.

It was a very cold winter in which the clothing of the river drivers would be hung up at night frozen stiff, and still stiff the next morning. The men put them on that way and stood by the fire until they thawed, Miller said.

The Maryville Times of April 8, 1899, reported 22 inches of local precipitation in the first three months of the year. The thaw of deep snow, the heavy rains and the washout of the splash dam left logs stranded along the bottoms from the Y to Rockford, with the consequence that Miller and his men spent most of the spring and summer dragging them back to the riverbed with ox teams. Some were poplars so large they weren't easily moved.

There were reports that the peak of the flood on Feb. 6 floated thousands of logs past the storage pond boom at the Roddy Branch sawmill, but a stockholder in the company denied it. "Some" logs were lost in the flood, he conceded.

The law and custom of the time was that a branded log remained the property of its owner, with the owner expected to pay 10 percent of a stray log's value to whoever salvaged it. It was also true that owners seldom recovered more than a fraction of the runaways, and the 1899 loss may have hastened the John L. English Co.'s departure from Little River. Downriver mills at Lenoir City and Chattanooga may have captured and sawed far more of the strays than English did.

But another group of investors soon would be looking secretly at Little River's upper prongs, with a view to building a logging railroad as a more dependable way to remove the timber.

Roy Myers said he was a "big kid about 10 years old" when he first helped his father drive cattle up one of the wilderness prongs in the spring. Sherman Myers had been taking his cattle to West Prong several years without owning the land. He built a cabin on the Defeat Ridge side of the valley, as a place for family members to stay when they went to see about the cattle. Friends also were invited to shelter there while they hunted bear and wild turkey, but were not welcome back if they left the iron cookpots unwashed and the place untidy the first time.

Because he left the premises in neater order than when he arrived, Will Effler was given a key to the cabin. When the Myers went to it after one of his visits, they found he had taken a laurel branch with several forks on it and

3

made a bucket rack. It was fixed so that the iron cookpots kept at the cabin could be hung upside down on the forks to drain, and thus not rust.

"Some of us boys would go up there and catch 75 to 100 speckled trout in two or three hours, before the loggers came," Roy said.

Hunters and livestock herders gave the ridges and creek branches of West Prong many of the names found on U.S. Geological Survey maps a century or more later. The Old Testament inspired some of the names, notably that of Eden's Garden Creek, with its grassy, open forest of oak and chestnut. Other names also seem to say that the local families were in awe of both the beauty and the rigors of the wilderness. Devils Nest Creek was slow traveling in places because of its jungle of rhododendron.

The Myers cattle were driven to the grass of Lower Chestnut Flats in April, when danger of snowfall was past. They were moved up the slope as spring and summer advanced, to Edens Garden, Devils Nest, Long Cove, and Bee Cove Creek. (The mapmakers don't use apostrophes.) An early feast for the cattle was a patch of ramps about 25 acres in size between Long Cove and Bee Cove Creek.

Drawers Gap, a Myers shortcut between tributary valleys, earned its name when Roy hung his underwear on a sapling there after the elastic broke. The drawers stayed while wind and storms tattered them to strings, and the mapmakers did write in the name of Drawers Gap.

Roy said his father could have owned part of that range, on the north slope of Thunderhead Mountain, if he had filed claim and paid the small tax that would have been assessed. But Sherman did not then foresee that West Prong's great forest would soon have value enough to make the taxes insignificant, or that a way could be devised to haul the timber out of the valley. Too, Sherman Myers may have regarded the West Prong as an idyllic landscape from which the timber would never be cut, a place of abundant water to which he and his sons would forever drive their cattle hungry for grass in the spring, to lead them home fatter in the fall.

– National Park Service photo

A log slide built by the Shea brothers on West Prong. The longest of these was two and a half miles long, and contained lumber enough to build several houses.

In mid-April of 1901, when Blount County men rescued a party of surveyors from a late, deep snowfall and freeze on West Prong, it became known locally that the valley was being staked for a big-time timber harvest. The leader of the surveyors was W.B. Townsend of Clearfield, Pa. Townsend would be president of the Little River Lumber Co. to be founded later that year, and the town around the new, two-band lumber mill would be named for him. The post office, which up to then had been named Tang, was also re-named Townsend.

The company put a standard-gauge logging railroad up West Prong and Laurel Creek, much of the

It was owned by Townsend teacher Georgia Bradshaw and called the Bradshaw House at the time of this 1989 photo. It was one of three built early in the century by the Shea brothers, logging contractors for Little River Lumber Co., and is said to have been occupied by the John F. Shea family in its first years.

There were many stream branches and many trestles on West Prong and Laurel Creek, and washouts of the roadbed were common. The present motor road to Cades Cove intersects this scene, where Bose Bryson's engine fell through in 1904.

latter on the grade of what is now the national park's motor road to Cades Cove. The Shea brothers, Tanbark Jim and Logger John, were hired as contractors, to furnish the timber-cutters, the horse teams and drivers. There were no steam-powered overhead skidders on West Prong.

The Sheas built log slides, one of them two and a half miles long, to bring timber from the upper valleys to railside. The slides were V-shaped troughs made from a combination of hewn and sawed timbers. So much lumber was used on one slide that it would have built 15 to 20 six-room houses, Roy said. But the slides were easier on horses than jay-bar, pole-road skidding would have been.

The Sheas worked on West Prong about five years, and left it slightly less ravaged than cable skidders would later leave the other prongs of Little River. But the brush and trash trees that grew in the wake of logging made a thicket so dense, in Roy's words, that "a rabbit couldn't get through" between Eden's Garden and Upper Chestnut Flats. Raymer Brackin fished West Prong about 20 years after the Shea brothers left, and saw a number of trestles and log slides still standing.

The lumber company's push after leaving West Prong was to complete the railroad up East Prong to Elkmont. While that job progressed, the Shea brothers and their men moved to White Oak Flats, East Prong's first hollow on the right above the Y. They logged that to keep the sawmill in Townsend busy until the rails reached the timber stands under Clingmans Dome.

The lumber company ignored and bypassed Middle Prong temporarily, and Roy Myers said it was because of Will Walker's early refusal to talk about

selling his land. He had already let English cut some yellow poplar and ash on Middle Prong, most of that work done in the 1890s.

Because it owned the railroad right-of-way past the mouth of the valley, Townsend's company was thought to be willing to wait until Walker's land could be bought at a price more favorable to the company. It would be another 20 years before a railroad would be built up Middle Prong.

The Shea brothers left the employ of Little River before the railroad reached Elkmont. They next logged on New River, north of the main ridge of the Cumberland Mountains, and are known to have been on the new job in 1909, and possibly earlier.

Myers followed the Sheas to New River briefly, and there learned to "top

Roy M. Myers stood at the grave of his grandfather William in the Myers Cemetery in 1977. Roy remembered the grandfather, who died in 1895 when Roy was six years old. At Roy's own death later in 1977, their two lifetimes in Tuckaleechee Cove had spanned more than 156 years. As young men Roy and his brothers plowed with a mule most of the land pictured here, up to the Smoky Mountain foothills.

load," or unhook the tongs after a crane had swung a log to a rail car. He was hired after the man before him fell from a carload of logs. He was paid twice as much as he had been making. A day's work on a log train paid $2.50, while pulling a saw or other work in the woods paid $1.25.

His native valley lured him back in 1910, to Jakes Creek above Elkmont where he hooked tongs, top-loaded, braked a log train, and on Sunday afternoons returned to Townsend to join brothers Luke, Ollie, and Bill as militant players on the baseball team. Roy became a log train conductor and stayed with the Little River Lumber Co. almost to the end of its operations late in the 1930s. He then joined the millwright crew of the Aluminum Company of America at Alcoa, and was there until retirement in the 1950s.

To the many who came to him in his final years in the 1970s, at his Townsend home on the river close to his ancestral farm and birthplace, Roy Myers was an honored teacher and reciter of local history. As a boy and young man he had known the area's last survivors of the Civil War, all Union Army veterans in that mountain neighborhood. He had roamed the Smoky Mountain forests before the lumber companies came. He had a special affection for older people, and they returned it by teaching him. Because of Roy M. Myers we know much more about Little River in the 19th and 20th centuries than we might have known.

Trail of John L. English lost

Knox County archives show John L. English married to Cora Sledge in 1887, and elected a notary public in 1892. Old city directories in the McClung Collection show English as a lawyer, land title abstracter, and notary public in 1893 and 1894. There are gaps in the directories, but those available list him as a lumberman for the first time in 1897, and show the affluent Judge Hu L. McClung as a member of the English corporation. Deed books in the Blount County Public Library and the Sevier County Library show the company acquiring thousands of acres of land on both East Prong and West Prong of Little River. Later records show the same tracts transferred to the Little River Lumber Co. English's name disappears from Knoxville directories after the 1904 edition.

Lou knew mountain water

The log splashes terrorized some of the families of the lower valley of Little River, Norma Singleton Smith told her children and grandchildren in family history sessions.

A Mr. French, whose first name Norma didn't remember, was crossing the river on horseback at a ford when a flood from the dams hit. The horse survived, but French was swept downstream and drowned. His body was missing for a long time, until it was found lodged in a tree on the bank where the river left it, Norma said.

Norma was born in 1890 and so was between 90 and 100 years old when the grandsons recorded some of her memories in different sessions. She would have been less than 10 years old at the height of splash-dam logging.

Her parents were Margaret DeLozier and Dr. Jefferson Davis Singleton, who lived on the Maryville side of Little River. Their parents in turn lived on the Wildwood side, in the neighborhoods of Wildwood and Eusebia. There were no bridges on the lower river in the 1890s, except a railroad bridge below Rockford. People crossed the river in boats, or in wagons and buggies or on horseback, or by wading at a few shallow places which could become suddenly deep after a shower or a surge from a splash dam.

Norma and her younger brother Lester sometimes traveled without their parents to visit grandparents at Wildwood and Eusebia. Their mother would put them in the buggy and weight the vehicle with rocks, so that it wouldn't float away on a splash if one should come. Margaret Singleton would warn her children of the danger, and warn them again not to dawdle while crossing the river.

– Photo from Smith family

Norma and Lester Singleton at the age they were fording Little River by buggy at the time of splash logging. Norma Singleton Smith reached her 100th birthday on August 24, 1990. Her husband, A.B. Smith, died in 1969.

But the horse pulling the buggy was Lou, a mare that could be depended on to stand in the river and drink a long time at every crossing. The river of that era was clean mountain water, fit to drink and delicious.

Norma and Lester became impatient with Lou when she drank, and there were times when they gladly would have changed horses in midstream. "She'd stop and look around at us, and we couldn't do a thing with her. It'd take us most of a day to reach our grandparents' home at Wildwood," Norma said. "There were no telephones, and until we got home again, our mother had no way of knowing whether we'd made it."

2

Walker Valley:
the only world there was

Wiilliam Marion Walker and Nancy Caylor moved into the wilderness of
the Middle Fork of Little River the year they were married, in 1859.
They were the first settlers of what came to be known as Walker Valley.

A footpath was their link with the nearest settlement, in Tuckaleechee
Cove several miles downstream. The path was later widened till an ox and
farm sled could travel.

– Photo from Margaret Crabtree

*The parts for Will Walker's factory-made wagon were carried into the valley and
assembled, because there was no road from the outside wide enough for it. The
short road that began and ended in the valley may have been built by the English
Lumber Co. for access to a splash dam above the mouth of Spruce Flats Branch.
Walker is in the picture, pulled by his durable ox Old Berry, given the name
because of his blackberry color.*

Will Walker and Nancy Caylor in their final years. She is the wife buried beside him in Bethel Cemetery at Townsend.

By the time he was 10 years old, Howard Taft Stinnett, born on Middle Fork in 1909, was carrying eggs and honey to sell to Art Emert. It was more than a seven-mile walk one way. Stinnett was photographed in 1990 at his home in Blount County.

This is from a letter written to me in 1956 by the late Emma Barnes, of Sunshine. She described herself as a niece of Walker, close to the family and its history.

Walker cut yellow poplar trees and hewed the logs to put up the house when they first moved into the valley. It was a home that sheltered them for all 60 years of their marriage, until his death in 1919 and Nancy's death three years later.

Walker was born in Tuckaleechee Cove at what is now Townsend. He was called Will by friends and family, and often called "Big Will" to set him apart from other, smaller William Walkers. He was the son of hardy parents, his father William C. Walker a frontier blacksmith, and his mother, Mary Ann Myers, a midwife on horseback. Emma Barnes called Will Walker "a great hunter and a good manager."

Will and Nancy moved upstream into the isolation of Middle Prong about two years before the start of the Civil War. Many of their former Cove neighbors were soon in the fighting, most on the Union side. Will stayed home and took some teasing to the effect that he had done so to run after the women, although there is no suggestion that he was looked upon as a slacker.

Roy M. Myers, who developed a friendship with Walker that lasted to the latter's death in 1919, said he teamed up with Jake Lawson during the Civil War years, to go house to house and cut firewood for people who had nobody at home able to do it for them. Wood was the only fuel for cooking and heating, and that was true even in the cities. Myers discussed his and Walker's friendship in conversations recorded by the writer in 1977.

After the war's end in 1865, Will and Nancy had more than 30 years in which few outsiders were aware of their life in the wilderness, and few coveted their mountain acreage with its private waterfalls and stands of giant timber. Then, at the beginning of the 20th century, logging railroads came to the West Prong and the East Prong. Middle Prong would have been a more accessible valley for a railroad, but Walker wouldn't sell.

He is said to have vowed from the first that he would never sell his land to the lumber companies. But before a railroad came to Tuckaleechee, Walker did tolerate splash logging from upriver property that adjoined his, and is believed to have sold limited amounts of yellow poplar and valuable ash timber from his land late in the 19th century. Ash and poplar are relatively light and buoyant woods, qualities that adapted them to splash logging.

A few other families came gradually to the valley to live on Walker's land, most of them in a tenant arrangement. They built log houses, barns, corncribs, and smokehouses, and cleared areas for gardens and cornfields. Walker was skilled at hewing and notching logs, and his legendary strength would have been in demand when buildings were raised. So that each of the scattered homes would be close to a supply of cornmeal, he built three water-powered grist mills. He shaped the millstones without outside help, and was able to sharpen the grinding channels of a millstone when it became worn.

Howard Taft Stinnett, revisiting his native valley in 1990, recalled that meal from the mills was his family's staff of everyday life. Wheat couldn't be grown easily and there were no big, smooth floors on which to thresh it. White flour for biscuits had to be carried from a store or mill in Tuckaleechee Cove, so that biscuits for breakfast were a special treat reserved usually for Sunday mornings. Cornbread was the fare three times a day most other days, and corn was the vital crop for every family in the valley.

Stinnett remembered more than 100 stands of bees in the yard of the Walker home on the east bank of Middle Prong, later the area of the Tremont Environmental Education Center. As a younger man Walker also kept dozens of stands of bees at the Blowdown, more than four miles walking from his home. The family made beehives from sections of hollow blackgum log, and burning and scraping the inside of a "bee gum" was a winter chore by the open fire. When the bees began to swarm in May and June, the new gums were rinsed inside with water flavored with fresh peach tree leaves and honey, to give them a welcoming aroma.

Walker did most of the taking of honey from the hives, usually without a mask or smoke. He would fill his mouth with honey and water, and lean back to spew it upward so that it fell in a spray on his head and shoulders. The

11

bees then seemed to forget their anger at being molested and would feed off him rather than sting him. Walker was the unquestioned master beekeeper of the valley, and the others deferred bee problems to him. Stinnett said the two mandatory times for robbing the hives of honey were after the yellow poplars bloomed in spring, and after the sourwood bloomed in July. The poplar comb is dark in color, and sourwood is sometimes very light, Stinnett said.

Walker sold tons of honey through the years, much of it hand-carried to merchants in Tuckaleechee. A 10-pound can sold for 80 cents to a dollar wholesale. After the Little River Railroad was built past the mouth of the valley, weekend visitors from Knoxville and Maryville came to the Walker door to buy. It was about a four-mile walk from where they got off the train at the Y, where the three mountain forks of Little River meet above Townsend.

Photo from Laverne Farmer

William M. Walker close to the end of his life, with his muzzle-load rifle, Old Death. He claimed to have killed 100 bears with it, a total that may have been an understatement. Walker was a lover of wilderness who kept his own forests on Thunderhead Prong intact until his death.

Whole families came for the entertainment of meeting Walker, to see him leap upward and click his heels together twice before landing, to hear his hunting stories and see his muzzle-load rifle, "Old Death." Will was so renowned a sharpshooter that he and his rifle were often barred from many shooting matches where prizes were given.

At least a few visitors were self-appointed missionaries who came to preach to him about his having children by more than one woman. There were more than 20 children through the years, including three by wife Nancy. In direct dealings with his children, whoever their mother, he is said to have acknowledged all of them as his own, and to have had a kind and fatherly relationship with most of them. He seldom discussed his extended family with critics of his lifestyle, except to remind them of Biblical patriarchs who had children by more than one wife. In his years of good health, Walker was able to send several daughters to

Maryville College, and one returned to the valley to teach in the school that was started in 1901.

Until a fungus blight began to kill the chestnut trees early in the 20th century, there were more of them than any other kind of hardwood tree in the Little River basin. The chestnut tree was regarded as a never-fail food source for wildlife, and Walker also counted on its autumn bounty to fatten his hundred or so hogs that roamed the mountainsides. The tenants may have had that many more.

"When hogs got fat on chestnuts, that was better than on corn. The meat had a better flavor," Howard Stinnett said.

"They had smokehouses. They would butcher the hogs and salt them down in the smokehouses. When the hams cured out, they would put them in what we would call bran sacks—cotton sacks. They would hang them then in the smokehouse.

"Then the side meat—they had a big table there and they would salt the sides down, or cure them or smoke them, or whatever. Then they would stack them one on top of the other after they got cured out. You could go out there any time and cut off a piece of side bacon five or six inches through, lean meat, and put it in a big kettle of beans and you had something good to eat."

Most of the families kept chickens that also foraged in the woods for most of their feed, and roosted in the trees at night. A surplus of eggs could be sold or bartered at Art Emert's store at Townsend, carried there six to eight dozen in a basket slung over the arm. The wholesale price was 16 cents a

– Photo from Marjorie Ownby

Walker Valley school was started in 1901, but date of the picture is uncertain.

13

In 1990 it sat unused and unnoticed a few yards from where US 321 turns from Townsend toward Wears Valley. Early in the century it was a busy country store run alternately by Art Emert and Sam Laws. Honey, chestnuts, ginseng, furs, butter, and eggs were among the items bought here for cash or bartered for merchandise. The residents of Walker Valley were frequent patrons.

dozen in the World War I years, or a dozen could be traded for a pound of coffee. Live poultry sold for a dime a pound. White leghorns were the preferred breed of laying hen, but domineckers were more plentiful. All tried to hide their nests, and it was easier to hide them from people than from the big blacksnakes that lurked around the barns. A blacksnake could swallow a dozen eggs. A hen that did succeed in hiding her nest would soon come into the open with the brood of chicks she had hatched.

The mountain valley was such a bountiful provider that there was a constant demand for more storage containers. Several in the community wove baskets from white oak splits, and Walker was regarded most skillful at making watertight barrels and kegs for storing kraut, pickled beans, and apple cider vinegar for winter. In the early years he made the oaken buckets for carrying water from the spring above the house. From visits to hardware stores in Maryville through the years, he had carried back a versatile collection of hand tools for working with wood, iron, and stone. His homemade blacksmith's forge had a forced-air draft from a bellows that was also homemade, of soft leather and wood.

Apple orchards were the most successful fruit orchards, and apples were sliced and dried or sulphured for storage every fall.Peach trees would bear only a few years before dying, but new trees were planted to offset the loss. Peaches were also sliced and dried in the sun.

14

Walker's main income was probably from trading cattle. Beginning in the safer years after the Civil War, he ranged through Wears Valley and Waldens Creek in neighboring Sevier County, buying cattle and driving them home on foot to Middle Prong. Even in the virgin forest of Thunderhead Prong there were places where great old trees had fallen in storms, and the sun had been let in to make the grass grow lushly. The cattle fattened there at no expense to him, and were brought down from the higher valleys to be sold to slaughterhouse livestock buyers in the fall.

Beginning about 1903, when the Shea Brothers began logging West Prong for the Little River Lumber Co., the farmers who had been ranging cattle on West Prong had to find other summer pasture, and some found it in Walker's wilderness. They came "in bunches," in Howard Stinnett's words, and Walker charged them a dollar a head for the season, from April until early September.

The cattle owners walked or rode a horse to the upper valley every week or so to look after their herds, and to replenish or relocate the salt. The cattle wouldn't wander far from their salt supply. Sherman Myers and a nephew, William A. Myers, rode up the valley regularly in the years before World War I. If they could leave their homes in Tuckaleechee Cove early in the morning, they counted on being back before dark. But they often camped for a night or several, in whatever three-sided lean-to they were nearest when evening came. Most of the shelters were located with the open end facing a rock against which a fire could be built.

The cattle relished the first greens of spring—the ramps, bear lettuce, turkey mustard, lamb's tongue, and crow's foot—after their winter diet of hay. And when the greens appeared, the residents of Walker Valley knew they would soon see the drovers. More than 70 years later, Howard Stinnett had it pictured in his memory.

"I'd be a little fellow out in the field, hoeing, and I'd just throw my hoe down and stand over at the fence and watch the cattle go by—there might be 500 head over a week's time, walking through there single-file. That was a show to me, you know. Back then I thought the valley was the only world there was. I didn't think there was anything else outside of there. A little kid raised in a place like that would look up at the hilltops and think that was a good-sized world.

"Old man Will Myers—he was called Pot Leg—he'd run cattle in there and he'd try to get in early, ahead of everybody else. He had 25 or 30 head in there and there came a big snow one spring, after he got them in there. He packed in a load of corn for his cattle, and they told on him that the cattle'd be standing in the snow and he'd offer one an ear of corn, and if it reached for the corn, Will wouldn't let him have it. He'd give it to one that wasn't able to reach.

"He pulled most of them through. He might have lost two or three. He had to haul corn in there two or three times before the snow melted.

15

"They'd run cattle in there before I was born, and I was born the eighth day of December 1909. They ran cattle up until Little River Lumber Co. bought that in there. And the valley that I was speaking of as being so big, it reached all the way over to the West Prong of the river, over toward Cades Cove. That was thousands of acres, which we called the Blowdown Prong but is also called Thunderhead Prong."

The sale of bearskins, 'coonskins, and other wild animal pelts, taken in traplines and from his skill with the antique rifle, were another reason for Walker's prosperity. Fur buyers came to the valley and carried away the hides in tow sacks loaded onto pack horses. The load was as narrow as possible to keep it clear of trees and branches that arched over the trail. Some buyers came on foot, and carried away the lighter hides threaded on long sticks balanced on a shoulder. The heavier bearskins were loaded onto pack horses.

Walker owned four or five big steel bear traps, homemade with the blacksmith skills learned from his father. They were sprung so strong that he hung a C-clamp close to each trap he set, so that if a man stepped into one he could use the clamp to hold the jaws open and free himself.

The traps were picked up before the start of cattle grazing season. One day after he had taken them up from the Devil's Courthouse, and was more than 70 years old and tiring, he hung the traps in a hemlock tree rather than try to carry them home. They weighed more than 60 pounds each.

– **Photo from Marjorie Ownby**
Ashley Moore, grandson of Will and Nancy Walker, hunted, trapped, and guided for most of his living. The big pelts hanging above him were coonskins. In 1938, Moore toured the East with a Grand Ole Opry troupe, playing a five-string banjo and singing his grandfather's hunting songs and Smoky Mountain ballads.

Walker didn't plan it that way then, but it was to be his last round of the bear traps. They were found by the lumber company's timber cutters nearly 20 years later. That stand of hemlock was one of the last to be logged.

A stroke disabled Walker in 1918, and a second one killed him on Dec. 30, 1919, when he was more than 81 years old. Two of his daughters left jobs in Knoxville to come home to care for him and Nancy in his final months. He had faded gradually before the stroke, unable to rob the beehives, run traplines, milk the cow, tend what hogs were left in the woods, or butcher them and put away the meat at hog-killing time. He had no beef cattle left in his final years. He and Nancy had been dragging long fence rails into the house and feeding one end to the fire without chopping them, because they weren't able to chop them.

The family story is that he was dying late in 1918 when he decided to accept the lumber company's offer for Thunderhead Prong, the stream that drains the northeast slope of Thunderhead Mountain and is one of the main feeders of Middle Prong. W.B. Townsend, president of Little River Lumber Co., came to the Walker cabin the day after Christmas, 1918. With Townsend was Sam H. Dunn, lawyer and notary public. The witnesses were two Walker daughters.

The deed on file in the Maryville office of the Blount County Register is for 96 acres "more or less," sold for $1,500 "in hand paid." Family members have said that Walker considered his acreage to be several times the deed figure. A family member said, "They sold it for a song, and the lumber company sang that."

For many years Walker had looked on Thunderhead Prong as being his, and loved its great poplars and hemlocks so much that he expected to the last to be able to save them from the Townsend band saws. A Walker daughter present the day of the sale recalled that he tried to exact a promise that Thunderhead Prong would not be cut, and she understood that a pledge was made to him that it wouldn't be cut. The promise was kept up to the time of W.B. Townsend's death in 1936, but the tract was cut a short time later.

If Walker could have been healthy a while longer, and hadn't been desperately short of cash for living expenses, he might have saved Thunderhead Prong as original wilderness for the Great Smoky Mountains National Park that would be created a few years after his death.

Will and Nancy both signed the paper with X's, although both had signed their names in other instances. The transaction was toasted with liquor from a jug Walker kept in a bee gum. His family said he seldom drank, nor had the making of whisky been one of his moneymaking enterprises, although some of the members of his extended family made and sold liquor. Stillhouse Hollow, across the river from the Walker home on the TVA topographic quadrangle, 157-NW, is a reminder of it.

Those who knew Walker doubt that he would have expected to be buried in a factory-made casket in a church cemetery outside his home valley, and be carried part of the way there by his own special funeral train provided by

17

W.B. Townsend. The family did look upon it as a thoughtful and generous gesture by Townsend. Some of the children now would be inheriting Walker's last big blocks of land, and the lumber company would be trying to buy it for access to the upper valley.

The gently-graded automobile road up the Middle Fork of Little River today makes it difficult to realize that the way out of Walker Valley could ever have been anything but easy. But the road follows the former roadbed of the logging railroad, and it hadn't been built when Walker died in 1919. Even the foot trail that led to the outside world didn't follow the river bottom, which then was an impassable tangle of rhododendron and boulder fields.

The family cemetery was on a knoll across the river from the Walker home, on two acres he had set aside for the purpose. Already there were several graves, and some of the coffins were said to have been hand-made by Walker. His own casket was bought at a Maryville funeral home by some of his children. It came by train to the Y, where the present motor road to Cades Cove splits off from the road up East Prong. The coffin was hand-carried the rest of the way, along the narrow mountainside trail to the cabin where Walker's body lay.

A number of people made their way into Walker Valley on the day of the funeral, and some of the younger men volunteered to be pallbearers, to carry Will in his coffin the four miles to the waiting funeral train. Roy Mack Myers and George LeQuire took the first turn, leading the funeral across the footlog that spanned the river in front of the Walker cabin. George Caughron and Will's nephew Jake Farmer were among others who helped.

Although he had been ailing in the months before his death, he was still a big man and a heavy load for a two-man carry, George at the front end and Roy at the back. The footlog did have a stout handrail on one side. There had been a storm in the upper valley and the river was up and raging, rolling its boulders as big as automobiles along in the current and cracking them together in ominous thunder. The funeral is believed to have been held on New Year's Day, 1920, although there were no records left in 1990 to confirm it. With the temperature alternating between freezing and mild that week, the trail was slippery.

Will was carried out by the same path he and Nancy had followed when they entered the valley in 1859. And now, 60 years later, she wasn't able to walk to his funeral.

When Nancy died in 1922, the logging railroad still hadn't been laid into the valley, and her funeral route was about the same as Will's had been. She was hand-carried the four twisting miles to the Y, and then borne by special train from the Y to Bethel Cemetery. Again, W.B. Townsend supplied the train, pulled by the graceful little Baldwin Pacific, No. 110.

An irony of Nancy's last years was that she was cared for by Will's daughters to another woman. It is said that they loved the woman they called "Mammy" Walker. They bought the casket and arranged for her to be buried beside her lawful husband, and finally Nancy had Will Walker to herself.

A mountain empire shrunk

Earl H. McCampbell said that William M. Walker became worried about losing his land sometime before World War I. The U.S. Forest Service at that time was moving to create a national forest in the Smokies, and negotiated to buy Walker's holdings, Earl said.

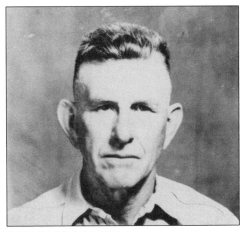

EARL H. McCAMPBELL

But Walker didn't have clear title to what he thought he owned, and the Forest Service wouldn't buy while it was clouded. Most people are aware that the national forest project for the Smokies was abandoned, and that a national park, instead, was established subsequently.

"He hired a professional engineer, R.C. Staebner, to do the surveying, and I worked for Staebner. I was what they called a 'tail pole' man. Every time they moved the compass, I'd hold the pole on the old mark so they could sight back on it," McCampbell said.

He helped Staebner survey an area two miles wide, mountain to mountain, and four miles long, and was told that Walker filed claim to it. There are 640 acres in a square mile, and so there were 5,120 acres in the eight square miles Walker was said to have claimed. The survey centered on Thunderhead Prong, on the Tennessee slope of Thunderhead Mountain.

He built a possession cabin in each section of his claim. Nobody lived in some of the cabins, but there was a patch of corn growing at each, Earl said. To grow a crop on a tract of land was considered proof of possessing it, he said.

Earl was aware that Walker later sold some of the surveyed property to Little River Lumber Company, but didn't know the details. He believed that Walker was "one of a very few" landowners in that part of the Smokies to be paid anything by the lumber company.

Before the company came in and built logging railroads up the valleys, mountain land with dense forest was considered of less value than land with open, grassy patches where cattle could be grazed.

Families who used certain areas for grazing might have an understood title to it, but didn't file legal claim to the land so they wouldn't have to pay taxes on it, Earl said. He said the lumber company filed its own original claims and paid only token amounts, if any, to those who had been living on the land or using it.

Walker, in his 80s, died in December of 1919, a year and four days after he had been paid for his Thunderhead property, but before the company began cutting its timber. The deed on file in the Blount County Courthouse

19

shows that he settled on the record for being paid $1,500 for 96 and a quarter acres. Members of Walker's family recalled in 1990 what a great disappointment it was to learn that he could prove ownership of only a fraction of the thousands of acres he thought he owned. Too, the family disagreed with his hiring of Staebner to make the survey. Staebner was forestry engineer for the lumber company, and the company was Walker's rival for ownership of the land.

Earl McCampbell was born in 1897 in what was then called Tuckaleechee Cove. As a boy and young man he had helped drive cattle to Defeat Ridge, Spence Field and Russell Field. Most of his working years were with the Aluminum Company of America at Alcoa, Tenn. In his final years he was retired, and lived on Little River at the lower end of Townsend.

John's new wilderness world

The clouds that give Thunderhead Mountain its name have poured historic storms into Middle and West Prong of Little River. The swollen stream thundering past their cabin door would tell the Walker family of such a storm on Thunderhead Prong miles above them.

The Walkers grazed their cattle in the wilderness of Thunderhead Prong in the warm months, and worried about them during storms. John Frank, born in 1860 and the first child of Will and Nancy Caylor Walker, was helping look after the cattle in his teen years.

It was on such an errand alone in 1875 that John stayed gone so long his father began searching for him. It was after the record storm that gouged new landmarks into the valley, and mowed a swath of giant poplars from a place that would thereafter be called the Blowdown. Travel was expected to be slow past flooded streams, in a valley without bridges or footlogs.

John returned safe. He explained his long absence with a story of having walked so far up Thunderhead Prong that there was no sign of anyone visiting there before him. He described it as a "New World" in his experience, and his family began to speak of the upper valley of Thunderhead Prong as "John's New World."

The loggers who invaded the valley in the 1930s looked on its magnificent timber in awe at the beginning, and they too called the place New World.

The story was told to writer Margaret Crabtree by Mary Alice Moore, a great-granddaughter of Will Walker. She said also that the place continued to be called "John's New World" well into the 20th Century, when the mapmakers shortened it to "New World." It appears as "New World" on the Thunderhead Mountain quadrangle, No. 157 SW, U.S. Geological Survey 7.5 minute topographic series.

3

Lonnie knew landmarks

The East Prong of Little River above Elkmont has more than 40 branches, each with a different name, and Lonnie Trentham knew them all and how to reach them on foot.

The headwaters of East Prong spring from the vast north slope of the highest ridge in the Smokies, from Mount Collins on the east to Cold Spring Knob on the west. The ridgetop along the Tennessee-North Carolina boundary includes Clingmans Dome, which at 6643 feet above sea level is the tallest of the Great Smoky Mountains.

Most of the names of streams and landmarks were bestowed by local people before the lumber company came to the upper valley. Elkmont itself is a newer name, born in the 20th Century. The settlement was called plain "Little River" until about 1908, Lonnie said. Jakes Creek had always been Jakes Creek, named for Jake Houser.

It was in 1908 that Little River Lumber Co. completed a logging railroad up East Prong. The company built a commissary, a small transient hotel, a machine shop for keeping its rolling stock repaired, and houses for the families of its supervisors, trainmen and other workers. The company then gave the place the name of Elkmont, Lonnie said.

Elkmont is best known today for one of the largest and most attractive campgrounds in the Smokies. As this was being written in 1990, there were still a few summer cottages held by private leaseholders, most of the cottages built before the Smokies became a national park.

Lonnie was born at Little River on Aug. 12, 1904, before it became Elkmont. He and wife Mary lived at Seymour, at the foot of Bays Mountain near Shooks Gap, at the time of our last interview in August 1983.

Although he was very young when the railroad came to Elkmont, he remembered some of it. His father's people, the Trenthams, had already lived there four generations.

When he was a boy, Lonnie listened to the old folks, including his patriarchal grandfather, Levi Trentham. It was directly from his family and his neighbors that he learned the lore of his native valley.

Bib overalls were his everyday apparel when Lonnie Trentham caught the 24-inch rainbow trout in the 1930s, at the mouth of Laurel Creek below Elkmont.

When he was old enough to gather stick-bait and help carry trout, Lonnie would go with his father, Phares Trentham, on fishing trips. Phares knew the remote streams where his favorite native speckled trout could still be found. The son was educated early in the names of all those places, and how to reach them.

Lonnie remembered a day on Goshen Branch, a tributary of Fish Camp Prong, when his father and Uncle Jonas Trentham caught more

Lonnie as a child didn't yet know overalls. His mother, Peggy Stinnett Trentham, made most of his clothing, including the "knee britches."

than 150 speckled trout and kept all of them, there being no limit on keepers then. "Most were small, but we carried them home, and I'll bet every one of them was eaten," Lonnie said.

Rainbow trout were brought up Little River and stocked for the first time in the second decade of the century, Lonnie said. After the railroad was built the rainbows were brought on the train in big cans. He said he liked to catch the rainbows and enjoyed eating the catch, but with Lonnie they were never more than second to the native speckled trout in all departments.

"Speckled trout don't have any scales. I can clean them about as fast as you can hand them to me," he said.

Mary Atchley Trentham didn't share her husband's fondness for trout fishing. She went with him "one time only," right after their marriage on May 19, 1923. Lonnie was working for Little River Lumber Co. then, in the logging of Battle Branch.

Mary said she couldn't keep up with him, leaping boulders, and had no desire to try again in the next 60 years of their marriage.

Logging ruined the fishing in some valleys for a long time, so much trash and dirt washed into the streams. "But we always had places to go, above where the timber had been cut. Like above the falls on Wilson Branch. There were trout up there—big ones," Lonnie said.

His knowledge of local geography helped him get work with a U.S. Geological Survey team that came into Little River Valley early in the 1930s, after it was taken into the Great Smoky Mountains National Park. He was hired as an ax man and rod man on the survey team.

He was also the man his foreman, Ed Bishop, turned to when he needed to know the name of a landmark. Somebody had told Bishop that Lonnie's answers would be reliable, that he was one of several who knew the Elkmont neighborhood best.

He said he didn't invent names and didn't need to. He could not have contrived names any more colorful than those already given to the creeks, hollows and ridges. But he was surprised recently, on reading a topographic map, to learn that one of the names he gave Bishop wasn't spelled like he had spelled it.

The middle fork of Three Forks, high on the north slope of the Smokies just west of Clingmans Dome, had always been Spud Tongue Branch to Lonnie. But there on the U.S. Geological Survey map, Silers Bald Quadrangle, it is called Spud TOWN Branch.

"Maybe Ed Bishop misunderstood me. I know it ought to be Spud Tongue Branch," Lonnie said. The stream was named for the business end of the tanbark spud that was used to peel bark from hemlock logs.

Lonnie soaked up so much lore of the mountains and of the logging camps that his friends, including his brothers and sisters and his five children, were forever saying, "You ought to write a book."

Lonnie said if he hadn't waited so long he would write one and it would include an account of how his father, Phares Trentham, along with John and

Big log was a yellow poplar taken from Poplar Branch of Jakes Creek in 1909. It was about 16 feet long, and diameter may have been seven feet or more.

Otha Ownby, cut down what is believed to have been the biggest poplar tree ever cut in the Great Smoky Mountains.

Lonnie's grandfather Levi had an 11-foot crosscut saw, a two-man saw that was a foot longer than the biggest owned by the lumber company. The 11-foot saw was so big that it was difficult to carry through the woods.

The three men borrowed Levi's saw, and even it was not long enough to cut through the swollen butt without removing one of the handles.

But after they had chopped a lead and sawed all the way through, the tree would not fall. It was a scary predicament and none of the measures they could think of would make it fall. So they left it standing on its stump as they went to their homes that night.

The wind did blow it over and thus finished their job safely for them sometime during the night. The butt log was so big and heavy that it could not be loaded onto a flatcar with a steam-powered American log loader. So they drilled holes in the log and blasted it apart with charges of black powder, to break it into sections that could be hauled to the mill at Townsend.

It happened on Poplar Branch of Jakes Creek when that valley was logged in 1909 for the first time, along its lower reaches.

4

Bad news for squirrels
when Walter bought a shotgun

Walter Cole was 17 years old and slight of build when he swung a nine-pound hammer for Little River Railroad beginning in 1907.

The superintendent watched him awhile one day when the road reached the Y, where the mountain forks of Little River flow together above Townsend.

Walter was swinging with a little more vigor than usual, in the presence of the top boss. He wanted very much to show that he could do the job, which paid 50 cents a day for 10 hours.

"Don't work so hard, kid. You'll give out," the superintendent cautioned him.

After which Walter settled into a pace that would let him last until the line was completed, into the Great Smoky Mountains above Elkmont. That was in 1909.

Then he asked for a job in the woods, cutting the big trees and getting them to the rail lines which soon were strung up almost every hollow in Little River's upper watershed.

The two biggest trees ever cut in that operation were two

– Vic Weals photo

Walter and Nancy Cole at home in Gatlinburg in 1978. Their first home together was on Fish Camp Prong above Elkmont in 1920.

poplars that grew on the divide between Jakes Creek and Little River near Elkmont. One was 29 feet in circumference at stump level and the other was 30 feet around.

The two-man saw used to cut them was 11 feet long, the longest available. And there wasn't much blade to spare at either end.

A teamster mounted his pair of big logging horses to the bigger stump and had the team do a complete swingaround on the stump, to show that it could be done.

Those two trees became Little River folklore. "We called them the Granddaddy and the Granny," Walter says.

The last logging Little River Lumber Co. did was on Middle Prong and its tributaries, through the last of the 1920s and into the 1930s. Walter carried the same 11-foot saw to a giant chestnut tree in that valley. A six-foot saw was standard equipment.

But before they cut the chestnut they found that it was hollow. So they let it stand, until the blight killed it completely.

Walter and all three of his brothers, Jess, Sid and Julius, worked for Little River at one time or another. Their father Alex worked there some, and for the people who logged the Oconaluftee Valley on the North Carolina side of the Smokies.

The sons worked some at what Walter remembers as the hardest job in the woods—ballhooting.

When a tree was cut on a very steep slope, they would peel the logs and nose them, round one end so that once a log was started sliding it would "ballhoot" to the foot of the slope by its own momentum.

The Coles lived in the Sugarlands then, on the West Prong of Little Pigeon River at the foot of the Huskey Gap Trail. It was the path they followed when they walked across Sugarland Mountain to their jobs on Little River after a Sunday at home.

When the boys were young they were sometimes allowed to follow their dad and help him when he guided visitors to Mount LeConte. That was before the trails were marked, and even before there were distinguishable trails, mostly in the years before World War I.

His wit and personality and considerable knowledge of his wilderness backyard made Alex one of the more sought-after native guides.

When Walter Cole cracked ballast rocks for Little River Railroad in 1907 it wasn't because he had to have a paycheck to survive. A young fellow in the mountains could and often did get along with almost no cash money in his pocket.

"But I wanted a shotgun more than I'd ever wanted anything. And nothing was ever given to you then. They couldn't. They didn't have the money.

"So I went down on Little River and helped build that railroad and got 50 cents a day for 10 hours.

"And I bought me a shotgun," Walter says.

"And I guess I've killed a boxcar load of squirrels with that old single-barrel Remington."

5

A railroad to remember

The highway that Great Smoky Mountains National Park visitors now travel, through Little River Gorge between Townsend and Elkmont, follows the former grade of a railroad that is almost universally admired by steam railroad fans.

In its nearly 17 years of operation, it may have been the most successful combination of logging railroad and scenic excursion railroad to exist in one place. Joseph P. Murphy as a young man was a principal architect of its uniqueness. Murphy left its employ several years before its 1925 closing.

Railroading was new to Murphy when he was hired for general office duties with Little River Lumber Co. in 1902. Meanwhile he was studying steam engines and locomotives, particularly those designed for logging railroads with steep grades and sharp curves. Soon he was being called upon to answer the related questions of other company managers, and soon he was given the title of railroad superintendent. Murphy worked with Baldwin locomotive designers to set the specifications for the line's two most famous rod engines, the small Pacific, No. 110, and the articulated Mallet, No. 148.

Baldwin delivered the 90-ton Mallet compound 2-4-4-2 in 1909. A Pacific-type engine, 4-6-2, the smallest Pacific built, was delivered in 1911. The latter became No. 110 and its prime run was with the daily mixed train to Elkmont. The more powerful No. 148 pulled the longer, heavier excursion trains on weekends, and log trains through the week.

Summer weekend passenger traffic was soon more than the capacity of the LRR mixed train, and Little River and Southern joined efforts to run a Sunday-only Elkmont Special. It was a through train running from Knoxville's Southern station to Elkmont with no change of cars, but with Little River's locomotives taking over from Southern's engines at Walland.

Before the two special rod engines were delivered, the company tried hauling excursions with its geared-drive Shay engines. The effect was something like running a modern passenger car in its lowest gear all day. The trips were hard mechanically on the Shay engines and annoyingly slow for crew and passengers.

Another sample of Murphy's affection for unique rolling stock was the 1912 Model T Ford touring car fitted with flanged wheels and converted to a rail car. The conversion was done in company shops at Townsend, a versatile facility that rebuilt at least three wrecked locomotives through the years.

The T Model was downbound from Elkmont one day when it didn't stop in time for locomotive No. 110 upbound. The little car bounced into the river and in the language of a later day was "totaled." It was replaced with a bigger Briscoe automobile with flanged wheels.

After Murphy left Little River, he became superintendent of Babcock Lumber Co.'s operations on Tellico River and Citico Creek, with band mills at Alcoa and Tellico Plains. Babcock's network of logging railroads required 10 locomotives, all hard-work engines manufactured at Lima, Ohio, under Shay patent. There were no show locomotives like the shiny, strutting Baldwins Murphy had put in service in his years on Little River.

He began work with Babcock in time to take a personal interest in the rebuilding of his new employer's Shay No. 2147, which had been wrecked and dismembered on Rough Ridge Creek in 1924. Repairs made it like new again when Murphy ordered a beauty treatment of green paint overall, with gold lettering and extensive gold striping.

No. 2147, after more tender-benders under several new owners through the years, is being restored again in the 1990s. It is in Townsend, maybe forever, as a display of the Little River Railroad and Lumber Co. Museum.

Murphy's favorite engine, the Baldwin Pacific No. 110, has been restored and hauls excursions for a museum railroad, Little River Railroad between Pleasant Lake and Angola, both in Indiana.

– Photo from Jack Foster

Joseph P. Murphy at the throttle of the 1912 Model T Ford rail car.

ECURSIONS TO HEART OF
SMOKIES
Little River Ry. Puts on Daily
Service Between Knoxville
And Elkmont.

The Little River Railroad Co., known
as the "Scenic Route," running through
the beautiful canyon of east prong of
Little river, will effective Monday, July
5, operate trains daily in connection with
Knoxville & Augusta railroad, Knoxville
to Elkmont and return, leaving Knoxville at 7:30 a. m., returning at 5:45
p. m. This makes an ideal trip right
into heart of great Smoky mountains
for rest and recreation during the hot
summer days.

J. P. MURPHY, Superintendent.

Start of daily train service from Knoxville's Southern Station to Elkmont was announced in the Journal and Tribune of July 2, 1909.

– Don Henderson photo

Elkmont visitors before World War I were proud to be photographed with shiny new No. 110.

– Photo from Stella McNiell

Locomotive No. 110 at the water tank in Townsend. In the cab was John Callahan, its first engineer, and high on the running board was Roy Cameron. Andy Hodge was on the ground at center, and Pruett Myers stood on the toeboard. Myers was killed in the fighting in France in World War I.

– Vic Weals photo

Shay locomotive No. 2147 on display at Townsend, Tenn., on a site where the Little River Lumber Co. band mill formerly stood. Before and after it first came to Little River in the 1930s, the engine was owned by the Babcock lumber companies, Bond-Woolf Co., Craig marble quarries, Conasauga Lumber Co., and Graham County Railroad.

Photo from Joe P. Murphy, Jr.

The Baldwin Mallet engine No. 148 pulls the Sunday morning excursion from Knoxville to the Wonderland Club stop at Elkmont. In another five minutes it will end its run at the Appalachian Club station, a mile away.

– Vic Weals photo

After Smoky Mountain Railroad between Knoxville and Sevierville was abandoned, No. 110 rusted at Shooks Gap through the 1960s, and souvenir hunters stripped most of what was removable. Several would-be buyers were discouraged by the estimated cost of moving it, until the Bloom family solved the logistics of hauling it to northeast Indiana.

– Vic Weals photo

Terry Bloom (left) and Byron Gramling were two steam railroad fans making No. 110 look good again in 1989 in Indiana. The engine was hauling weekend excursions for another Little River Railroad, a museum railroad between Pleasant Lake and Angola.

6

A locomotive
that was fun to run

To "hostle" a locomotive was to work on it at night, empty the ash pans, clean the firebox of clinkers, refill the coal tender and water tender, load the sand reservoirs, oil several moving parts and sweep out the cab.

Sam Compton was hostler of the lumber company's two main Shay engines at Elkmont in 1918, but Sam would rather work at his trade of building houses. It was one of the reasons his 13-year-old son John was welcome to help with the locomotives, and for John it was the start of a life career.

No. 110 at Elkmont in 1918. John Compton was 13 years old and saw the photographer make the picture. Fireman Arthur Smith stood on the running board. Standing below, from left, were conductor Charles Clark, brakeman Luther Swann, and engineer John Callahan.

The engines were No. 9 and No. 11, both kept busy daytimes in the logging of Fish Camp Prong. Partly because of the steep grades in that long valley, the Comptons were careful to replenish the sand for traction each night.

There was a stove with a hopper on it in the machine shop, and they'd sift the debris out of the sand before loading it into the hopper. After it had dried on the hot stove, the sand was loaded a bucketful at a time into three reservoirs on each engine. The sand dome atop the boiler held 17 buckets, as did each of two rear reservoirs. The sand was for trickling onto the rails to give the wheels braking traction.

John learned to clean the fire, which was to remove the clinkers, and after that it was easy to keep the fire going all night. John was sent home about 11 p.m., where his mother, Mary Elizabeth Reagan Compton, had a late supper on the table for him.

His dad stayed with the engines, keeping the fires going, until their crews came next morning to take them up the valley. One of his final chores was to blow the whistle of one of the Shays—four long toots to signal 4 a.m., getting-up time for most families in the camp.

The Comptons stayed at Elkmont one summer before moving back to Townsend, and young John was soon on the payroll as a night watchman over the company's three rod engines, 110, 148, and, part of the time, 105. He worked there more than three years, until he was old enough to be hired as extra brakeman or extra fireman.

He learned to prefer not to be assigned to one of the Shay engines. A Shay's tender held seven tons of coal, enough for one day, to be tossed into the firebox a shovelful at a time. "A Shay was slow, and firing or running a Shay was hard work. I didn't like them, but I did like a rod engine, something that would get up and go with you," John said.

His first regular firing run was with the Baldwin Mallet, No. 148 to Elkmont, pulling empty flatcars upbound and heavy log trains downbound. Woody Dew, engineer of 110 at the time, pulling the daily mixed train to Elkmont and hauling trainloads of finished lumber from Townsend to the connection with Southern Railways at Walland, meanwhile was using his influence to have John as his fireman. It was the years with Woody in the cab of 110 that John remembered most pleasantly.

"You could take that old 110 and get up a load to hold her down and making about 35 or 40 mile an hour and she'd really talk to you," John said. "She had a loud exhaust. That thing, up that river going to Elkmont, pulling hard, that exhaust would crack like a .45 pistol, echoing from the cliffs. There was just the railroad and the river in that gorge, and the railroad was right beside the river."

Woody Dew's wife, Flo, became superintendent of Little River Railroad after the departure of Joseph P. Murphy in the early 1920s, and the Dews became John Compton's family. They lived near each other in the Townsend hotel the lumber company had built beside the railroad.

If somebody died who worked for Little River Lumber Co., there'd be a funeral train pulled by No. 110. Even after the undertakers bought big, long motor hearses, the train was a more stately ride to the cemetery.

If it was a logger or member of his family who died, the train would take the mourners to the funeral, and take them back up the river to their shanty car homes and their jobs.

When W.B. Townsend's first wife, Margaret Townsend, died on New Year's Eve of 1923, No. 110 was draped in black to haul the funeral train to Knoxville, where she was buried in Old Gray Cemetery. The engine was regarded as Margaret Townsend's pet, and her portrait was painted on one of the cab windows.

J.K. Foster was the locomotive's fireman on several funeral runs through the years, as his son Jack was following him. Jack started his engine career as fireman on No. 110 in 1921, and later was its engineer after it was sold to the Smoky Mountain Railroad. Jack or his father or both were in the cab for many of the years the engine ran in East Tennessee.

Oliver Gilland started firing on a Shay, No. 9, when he was 17 years old, and was running No. 110 in 1939 when Little River Railroad was in its last days. Oliver began work with the Aluminum Company of America at Alcoa, Tenn., in September of 1939, and that was the end of his railroading career.

– Foster family photo

The picture is of both Fosters in the cab of No. 110 at Townsend in the early 1920s. Son Jack is at left in the doorway, and J.K. Foster, the father, is at right. We don't know who the boy between them was. Standing this side of the engine was brakeman Luther Swann. A portrait of Margaret Townsend, first wife of Little River Lumber Co. president W.B. Townsend, is dimly visible on the cab window. The engine pulled her funeral train.

At his home in Townsend in 1990, he still enjoyed talking about his mountain railroad years. Because he was one of the last survivors of those who had run the old Babcock Shay, No. 2147, railroad fans came regularly to his door to bask in his memories. No. 2147 is the Shay that is parked beside the Parkway in Townsend, as a museum exhibit of the resurrected Little River Railroad and Lumber Co.

John Compton worked for Little River about 16 years, to September 1936. He went to jobs in Ohio and Kentucky, and briefly to the Clinchmore Coal Co. mine on New River. He didn't like coal mining and went back to railroading, first at Oak Ridge during the war, then with the Smoky Mountain Railroad between Knoxville and Sevierville from 1951 to 1961, and finally with the engine Klondike Kate at what became Dollywood.

John Compton regretted the passing of steam locomotives and the introduction of diesels. "But a man has to take whatever comes," he said.

"If you'd sit in that racket (diesels) all day you couldn't hear when you'd get off. You'd be in the middle with a big diesel motor at each end—a solid roar all day long. You couldn't shut them down except to check the motors.

"A steam engine is quiet when you stop it, and steam engines will just go on forever. But a diesel is like an automobile—they give a lot of trouble. At Oak Ridge they had diesels in the shop all the time, being worked on."

John continued to contribute to this book up to the final months of putting it together in 1990. His home in retirement was at the foot of Chilhowee Mountain in the Cold Spring Community, within whistle echo of the former Walland terminus of Little River Railroad.

Mountain railroads required many trestles and bridge piers. They were usually built of hemlock because it was most plentiful.

36

37

– Photo from S.P. McNiell

Little River's first rod engine, No. 1, couples to loaded log cars early in the century, on a siding at the Forks in what is now Great Smoky Mountains National Park above Townsend, Tenn. The logs had been brought out of West Prong and Laurel Branch by other engines better adapted to sharp curves and steep grades. Because it was awkward on curves, No. 1 once left the tracks near Walland and plowed into the river upright.

Luther "Big Smoke" Waycaster earned the nickname from the trademark plume of black smoke on the engines he fired. Luther was shoveling into the firebox of No. 110 as it steamed into Elkmont on the day of this picture.

Jenkins family photo

The mountain grades of the headwaters of Little River required bushels of dry sand almost every working day, trickled onto the rails to give traction to the geared-drive Shay locomotives. The switchback pictured was a common engineering device for overcoming steep grades.

7

Portraits of logging were Shelton's legacy

James B. Shelton was born on Shelton Laurel, the mountain forest named for his family on the French Broad River in Buncombe County, N.C. But Jim lived most of his more than 90 years in Tennessee's Little River Valley and nearby Wears Valley, and it was there that he became interested in photography early in the 20th Century.

Jim's equipment was a bulky bellows camera with rectilinear lens. It made negatives on sensitized glass plates five by seven inches in size, with a special dark slide allowing two postcard-size pictures on one plate. Jim climbed mountains, leaped boulders and crossed rivers with his camera to record a picture history of the logging era.

There was no electricity in his darkroom and his printing light burned kerosene. One of his children, daughter Effie Shelton Phipps, says all of his prints were contact prints, the negative held against the paper in a frame, and the frame facing the open light of the lamp while Jim counted off the seconds of exposure.

"I watched him a lot, and I remember that if he left it exposed to the light too long, the print would be too dark," Effie says.

She says her father's darkroom plumbing was a trough that carried water from Little Brier Creek into the room. He washed his negatives and prints in the water of the trough. Another daughter, Hazel Hembree, says the darkroom she remembers was on runners, like on a farm sled, so it could be moved easily.

The big activity in that part of the Smokies then was with the Little River Lumber Co. Shelton's several jobs with the company included one as a "track walker" and later as a track maintenance foreman on the railroad. He was a member of the crew that built the Long Arm Bridge, on the company's main line up Little River Gorge from Townsend to Elkmont.

Effie says photography was a hobby and sideline for her father and never his main way of earning a living.

"He enjoyed taking pictures. He didn't try to collect money for a lot of the pictures he made," Effie says. Whether or not Shelton was aware of it at the time, his pictures often said more than words can say about the Little River logging era.

He was out one Sunday with his family when he decided he'd set up camera and tripod to photograph the "swinging railroad bridge" across Little River at the mouth of Meigs Creek.

The bridge was built somewhat like a footbridge. Most of the support came from steel cables suspended across the river just under the wooden crossties that held the rails. There were guy cables, not visible in the picture, to keep the bridge from swinging side to side.

No standard locomotive ever crossed the bridge. An incline engine was hauled to the top at the beginning, and used thereafter to lower carloads of logs at the end of a cable by controlled gravity. After the logs were dumped beside the main railroad, the empty cars were winched to the top again.

The incline engine was similar to one manufactured by the Surrey-Parker Co. of Pinetown, N.C., according to lumber industry historian Fred C. Babcock. Those who worked around the machine on Meigs Creek affectionately called it the "Sara Parker."

Shelton's camera recorded the only known "swinging" railroad bridge. It spanned East Prong of Little River below Meigs Falls early in the 1920s.

The Surrey-Parker included a crane boom for lifting logs to the car, which was a smaller car than a standard railroad flatcar. The standard cars were about 36 feet long while the incline cars were about 18 feet. Most of the logs cut from bigger trees in the Smokies were a few inches over 16 feet long.

If the day hadn't been Sunday, Jim Shelton's picture might have included a loaded log car being lowered across the bridge.

The picture we have is a copy of a print saved more than 60 years by Lavern Massey of Wears Valley. Lavern and her husband Jack lived at the swinging bridge awhile. She cooked for the workers at a boarding camp there, and Jack was engineer of a log train.

Lavern's picture had been torn top to bottom at the right of center, and we pieced it together to copy it. The bridge is important to the history of mountain logging because it may have been one of a kind.

Jim's photo of the dead chestnut tree is also a treasure from the past, a reminder of the great size the species sometimes reached before a fungus blight killed them all early in the 20th century.

Jim and his wife, Caroline Walker Shelton, were prominent in Little River folklore. Caroline was one of seven daughters born to John N. "Beaver" Walker and Margaret King in Little Greenbrier Cove. Caroline was the only Walker sister to marry, and her spinster sisters became famous for winning the fight to stay in their log home after their land was purchased by the new national park..

Photo by Jim Shelton in 1912 or 1913 shows homes of foremen and workers at Elkmont, outhouses, cowsheds, locomotive shed, and, nearly out of picture to the right, the island that is now Elkmont Campground in Great Smoky Mountains National Park.

Jim Shelton was the photographer and the biggest known chestnut tree in the Smokies was the subject. It stood below Tremont Falls, where the timber-cutters rejected it for lumber because it was hollow. Wife Carolne is at left; their son John looks out from the hollow; others are daughters Leona (Cotter), Effie (Phipps), and Hazel (Hembree). Shelton and crew eventually cut the tree and used the logs in a retaining wall, when the railroad was built above Tremont in 1925.

8

When death had the last dance

The railroad from Townsend to Elkmont was completed in December of 1908. The first trainload of logs from above Elkmont was delivered to the sawmill at Townsend in January of 1909.

Timber cutters had been at work in the valleys above Elkmont for several months. Horse teams snaked logs out of the hollows and down from the slopes as they were cut, and left them to weather until rails could be laid to where they were stockpiled.

By June of 1909 there was a steady daily movement of timber to the mill from Poplar Branch in the lower watershed of Jakes Creek, across from the upper end of what is now Elkmont Campground in Great Smoky Mountains National Park.

JOHN C. FARMER

John Coy Farmer was 23 years old and a bookkeeper at Cross Mountain Mine, above Briceville in Campbell County, when news of big events in his native Little River Valley lured him back in 1909. Farmer began working for the lumber company in April and opened the Elkmont commissary, or company store, on April 19. Several years before Farmer's death in the early 1960s, he put into writing some of his memories of the excitement at Elkmont in 1909.

Everyday service from Knoxville to Elkmont began on July 5 with a crowded train and a great outpouring of local people to meet it. Some of the locals were company employees and their wives and children, and some were families who had long lived on Little River's upper reaches or across the mountain in the Sugarlands above Gatlinburg. Farmer said the commissary sold 30 gallons of ice cream that day and ran out.

Aside from picnicking, strolling, and bathing in the mountain river that was cold even in July, the big excitement for the excursionists was a log train wreck still lying in a Jakes Creek ravine. It was the wreck that killed engineer Gordon A. Bryson and brakeman Charles M. Jenkins on June 30, less than a week before.

Bryson died under his locomotive in the Elkmont ravine at right.

Both Knoxville newspapers had stories next day of the Bryson and Jenkins deaths, but with little information about either man or his family. Seventy years later, with the help of Lois Vananda and Margaret Stephenson, we learned that "Daddy" Bryson was buried in Knoxville's New Gray Cemetery and that his full name was Gordon A. Bryson. Easier to find was the grave of brakeman Charles Jenkins, in the Myers family cemetery at Townsend.

Further digging into Lawson McGhee Library's microfilm files and records in the McClung Historical Collection showed that

Stone in Knoxville's New Gray Cemetery marks engineer Bryson's grave.

Gordon Bryson was a veteran former engineer with Southern Railways and its forerunner, the East Tennessee, Virginia and Georgia Railroad. Railroaders of the period were among Knoxville's working elite and generally well known to each other. Bryson's funeral was probably a big one, despite the scant notice in the newspapers.

Bryson and one of his sons, Bose, began working for Little River Lumber Co. almost at the start of operations on Laurel Creek and West Prong, and continued into the later logging of East Prong. Both were locomotive engineers for the company in 1904, and perhaps earlier.

A look back at the older Bryson, through the memories of those who knew him on Little River, showed that almost nobody was aware of his real first name. They called him "Daddy" Bryson to set him apart from his son, perhaps, but more likely because he was a fatherly figure who thrilled children by waving to them from his locomotive cab. He carried a quantity of nickels which he held out one at a time to logging camp youngsters. At ice cream suppers he was known to buy for children who otherwise would have gone without eating.

Bryson was nearly 55 years old at his death. Several local poets recorded the story in ballads, but none with audiences like "Casey Jones" and the "Wreck of Old 97" had. Bill Abbott composed "Daddy Bryson's Last Ride" to be sung to the tune of "Red Wing." Neither did those verses win their author a Nobel laureate.

Bill Cooper, later a Knoxville service station owner at Martin Mill Pike and Chapman Highway, was a boy at Townsend when the ballads were being written. Bill said Bose Bryson didn't like the song about his father and once drew a pistol on somebody who was singing it. Bose warned him to "never sing that song in my face again."

The 1910 city directory shows Bose Bryson living on Park Avenue in Knoxville, an indication that he left the employ of Little River Railroad soon after his father's death. Charles S. Dunn, Townsend native who was with the U.S. Forest Service in 1916, ran across him that year at Erwin, Tenn., where Bose then worked for Clinchfield Railroad. Ted and Nell Harrison inquired around Erwin in 1979 and found a few oldtimers who remembered that Bose lived on Love Street while he was an engineer for Clinchfield. His trail ends there, after we had followed it for years in the hope that he might have a photograph of his father.

Engineer Bryson and brakeman Charles M. Jenkins had been killed in the Elkmont wreck of the locomotive and five flatcars heavily loaded with logs. A theory

Robert P. Headrick of Wears Valley, one of three survivors of the 1909 wreck.

of the cause was that the sand reservoir was clogged, and without sand for braking traction the train ran away and left the rails on the steep downgrade.

Log loaderman Robert P. Headrick was one of three men who jumped from the train unhurt. Conductor Aaron Jones and fireman E.T. "Hoot" Foster were the others. Hoot is said to have earned his nickname from the way he blew a locomotive whistle, short blasts of hoot! hoot! hoot! Bob Headrick lived another 56 years, and most of the credible information we have about the wreck came from him before his death in 1965.

A working man's lunch box at that time was called a dinner pail or a dinner bucket, and those of the two dead men were found in the wreckage. Annie King Whaley said that when a logger was killed accidentally, it was custom to hang his dinner bucket to a tree in his memory. The Jenkins and Bryson lunch pails stayed there for years, Annie said. Her husband, Crockett Whaley, was a Little River logger.

Charlie Jenkins left the train, too, but was pinned against a rail by a large log falling from a car. He died of the injuries about the time his rescue train reached Townsend with J.K. Foster at the throttle. Jenkins' wife, Amanda, was able to buy a farm with the insurance settlement. Their daughter Maude was little more than a year old at her father's death. Their son, Charles M. Jenkins Jr., was born seven months after his father's death.

Charlie's brother Tom Jenkins died in 1915 under a pile of spilled logs on Huggins Branch of Hazel Creek, on the North Carolina side of the

Amanda Jenkins as a widow, with children Maude and Charles Jr.

Maggie Jenkins, widow of Tom, with their youngest child, Paul Eagle Jenkins.

Smokies. Tom's wife, Maggie, and Charlie's wife, Amanda, were sisters, and neither married again after their husbands' deaths. Tom and Maggie had four children, the youngest less than a year old at his father's death.

Boys too young for the very dangerous jobs in the woods were thronging to the lumber companies in nearly every valley in the Smokies, and it was unfortunate that many were being hired. Tom Jenkins, though, made it his mission to intercept the boys before they were hired, to try to convince them to go home and look for safer opportunities.

The Jenkins brothers and their wives, the Carver sisters, were graceful, energetic cloggers and dancers, a talent that sometimes saved the lives of Tom and Charlie when they stepped nimbly away from the many dangers of loading timber onto flatcars. Charlie was almost able to leap clear of the log that killed him on Jakes Creek. Tom had no chance to dodge the avalanche of logs that rolled over him on Huggins Branch.

Eagle Rose (left) and Tom Jenkins served in the Army together in the Philippines. They were together on Hazel Creek, N.C., the night before Tom was killed.

Amanda Carver and Charles Jenkins at their wedding in 1907, when she was 20 years old and he was 27.

47

CAUGHT BENEATH HIS ENGINE

Engineer Bryson Meets Death On Little River Road—Lost Control of Train on a Siding.

In an accident on the Little River railroad Wednesday afternoon, Engineer Bryson was caught beneath his engine when it was ditched from a siding and instantly killed. Another member of a logging train crew whose name could not be learned was fatally hurt.

The accident occurred on a siding several miles above Elkmont and from meager details received, it seems that the log train had been overloaded in strict violation of the rules of the company. Coming down a side track which runs back into the mountain, the track was so slippery from rain that the speed of the locomotive could not be controlled and when it struck the main line at the junction of the switch, the engine was ditched with the fatal result above mentioned.

The scene of the accident is beyond Elkmont from Knoxville, the line between Townsend and Elkmont, . . . rapidly becoming a favorite place for picnic and excursion parties.

A newspaper story of the wreck blamed the employees for overloading the train "in strict violation of the rules of the company." But foremen continued to overload the trains.

Second from left was lumber grader W.H. Linginfelter, who attended the funerals of Jenkins and Bryson and was a key to finding the Bryson grave 70 years later.

Old pictures were on the table as the children and grandchildren of Tom and Maggie Jenkins were reunited in 1979, 64 years after Tom's death in a log train wreck. The three surviving children were Clyde H. of Rochester, Mich., at center; his sister Iva Lee Jenkins of Rockwood, Tenn., next on right; and Paul Eagle Jenkins of Bradenton, Fla., at far right. All sampled life in logging camps on Little River and Hazel Creek.

Other wrecks

Wreck of No. 9 at the mouth of Rough Creek left its trainload of logs strewn along the right of way. Another view of the March 1914 wreck (below) shows No. 9's boiler with cab and running gear stripped away. It was rebuilt, and served more than 15 years before it was wrecked beyond repair in 1931 on Marks Creek.

Boiler and firebox are in foreground, torn from the frame of Little River Lumber Co.'s Shay locomotive No. 4 by an explosion in the boiler in 1914, on Little River above the mouth of Rough Creek. Fireman Sam McClanahan was burned fatally, but engineer Walter Hall survived. The explosion knocked young Arlie Maples from his perch on a nearby water tank where he was eating lunch. Maples later became engineer of No. 9, the engine at right showing scars of its recent wreck in the same vicinity.

Wrecked caboose is one that ran away and left the rails above Elkmont July 13, 1917. J.N. Badgett, Pleas Myers and Earl Dockery were killed, from injuries when they jumped or from the car's final plunge onto the boulders of Little River.

Little River Lumber Co.'s last two serviceable Shay locomotives, No. 9 and No. 11, were destroyed when they ran out of control down Marks Creek in April 1931. The boiler of No. 11, visible here in the ravine, was intact and was given to Townsend School to serve many years as a heating plant.

No. 11 Shay in a happier pose, long before the wreck on Marks Creek.

9

Just say 'no' to george-shooters

By the time Little River Railroad had pushed up East Prong to Elkmont and higher (1909), there was a considerable crowd of strangers in the Smokies. They worked beside the local men with ax, saw and peavey, with oxen and horses and an increasing amount of steam-powered equipment—log skidders and log cranes along with powerful geared locomotives.

"Wood hicks" was their name for themselves, for all those men who worked in the woods, Roy M. Myers said.

There were some who wouldn't miss a payday, who stayed with the job through snow, slush and miserable cold rain of late winter. But the commoner thing was for a logger to move around, or at least take an unpaid vacation now and then. There was a saying that there were three gangs in the logging woods—one arriving, one working, and one leaving.

ROY M. MYERS (in 1977)

Roy said he was so young and naive, when he first went to work for the lumber company, that the older hands were reluctant to tell him the facts of life. But his boss did warn him, first day on the job:

"Watch the george-shooters! They'll want you to take a snort with them, and it'll ruin you if you keep it up."

"George," Roy said, was what loggers early in the century called cocaine. It was as illegal then as it is now, and Roy said he tried it only one time.

Indians of the high altitudes of South America's Andes Mountains have chewed coca leaves for centuries, to give them endurance against the cold and thin atmosphere and to allay hunger pangs.

Cocaine is the potent, powdery extract of the same leaves, and some of the oldtime loggers, when snow was on the slopes and the thermometer below freezing, wouldn't go into the woods until they had sniffed a pinch of "George" up each nostril.

Not all of the loggers used it, Roy said. Because it was something they hadn't heard of at home, many local men were leery of it. But there were drifters and adventurers and even some locals who used it regularly.

Of all forbidden substances, liquor remained the most available, from local suppliers of homemade, illicit varieties after Tennesseans voted the state dry in 1909.

Closest place to buy cocaine was in Knoxville, on a section of downtown Central Street then called the Bowery. The price was $5—two days' wages—for a small tin box of it, about a two-week supply with careful rationing. An everyday george-shooter would quit his job to be free to go to Knoxville to replenish his supply.

10

Mary had a stingy little lamp

Mary Brackin was born in 1889 in the Smokies above Gatlinburg, in the Sugarlands about a mile below the Chimneys. When she was almost 16 years old she married H. Marshall Whaley, a neighbor boy who was two years older than Mary.

Marshall Whaley and Mary Brackin at their marriage in 1905. They had been together 61 years when he died in 1966.

Marshall farmed for a living in their first years together, and Mary helped him. "I put as much meat on the table as he did," she told people proudly. "I'd go up one hollow with a rifle and he'd go up another, and I'd come back with as many squirrels as he would."

It was her three brothers, Cicero, Andy and Riley Davis Brackin, who taught Mary to shoot. She was bragged about locally for her skill with rifle, pistol and shotgun.

"They set an egg up in the yard one Christmas, and I hit it first time with a .22 rifle," Mary said.

Early in the years of their marriage the Little River Lumber Co. laid its logging railroad to Elkmont and beyond, up the valley across Sugarland Mountain from where Mary and Marshall were living.

He liked to cook and so did she, and soon they crossed the mountain and started a boarding house for lumberjacks. Their building was several portable shanties joined together, beside the railroad at the mouth of Mannis Branch, on Little River below Elkmont.

The shanties were what Mary called "set-off houses," because they were brought to the site on railroad flatcars and "set off" with a log crane.

Mary fried the eggs and meat and made the gravy for their 25 to 30 boarders most mornings. Marshall baked biscuits from dough he had mixed the night before. His biscuits were what Mary called cat-head biscuits because of their size, cut from dough with the end of an empty tin can.

After supper at night many of the boarders, those who hadn't gone to bed, would sit around the stove in the lobby and maybe write letters, talk or listen to others talk.

Mary's lamp minus the brass wheel that her husband sawed off to save the glass chimney from being blackened.

The lobby's only light was from an oil lamp Mary had received as a wedding gift from her parents, Davis Brackin and Mary Josephine Cole Brackin. Mary's husband was known as a very "saving" person and he would keep the lamp wick low so it wouldn't burn much oil.

Coal oil, or kerosene, was what most people called it in that day. It cost 10 cents a gallon or less at Little River Lumber Co.'s Elkmont commissary.

Almost every time Marshall turned the wick down, one of the boarders would turn it back up. They'd accuse him of being too stingy to buy coal oil and he'd say it wasn't that at all.

"Every time you turn up the wick it smokes up the lamp globe, and I'm tired of cleaning the lamp every morning," Marshall would say.

Finally he thought of a way to make it more difficult for the boarders to turn up the wick. He cut off the little brass wheel by which the wick was adjusted.

With the lamp flame kept low the way Marshall set it, a dime's worth of coal oil would last a month or longer.

Mary and Marshall left the Smokies when their native Sugarlands Valley was taken into the new Great Smoky Mountains National Park in the late 1920s. They moved to Cleveland, Tenn., where they owned and operated a dairy farm, and for several years owned and ran a restaurant. They were successful at most of what they tried.

Marshall died there in 1966, after they had been married 61 years. Mary continued to live in Cleveland, close in friendship and in distance to families named Parton and Ownby, and others who also have roots in the Great Smoky Mountains.

Mary kept the lamp her parents gave her on her January 1905 wedding day. It had the original ornate globe, never broken nor cracked in more than 76 years, and it was still minus the little brass wheel.

Mary Whaley and Jack Ownby, a Cleveland, Tenn., neighbor and great-nephew with roots in the Smokies.

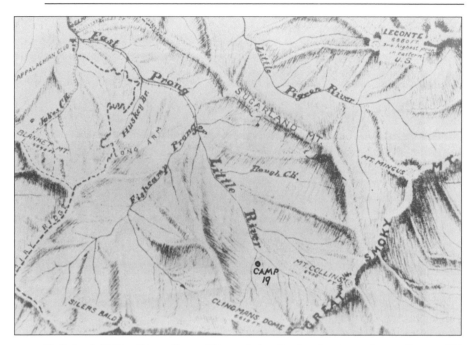

Relief of Little River from Elkmont to its headwaters shows Camp 19's approximate location. It was above Three Forks and below Clingmans Dome, highest mountain of the Smokies at 6,643 feet.

11

It's a long way to Tipperary from Camp 19 on Little River

Thousands of visitors to Gatlinburg in the half-century after 1930 have known Curtis McCarter personally. He and his family have been owners or partners in national park riding horse concessions for most of those years. But this story goes back further in time, to McCarter's stay at the highest of all logging locations of the Little River Lumber Co.

Early November of 1918 brought snow eight inches deep to the upper slopes of Clingmans Dome, highest of the Great Smoky Mountains. For that elevation it was no earlier than many snows that have fallen in other autumn seasons. McCarter worked in the 1918 snow at Camp 19 above Three Forks, on the Tennessee side of the mountain that rises to 6,643 feet.

He worked on the crew of a machine that brought logs down the slope on overhead cables, and dropped the logs in piles beside the railroad. Curtis was born May 28, 1900, and so was 18 years old in 1918 and expecting to be called almost any day in the World War I draft.

His greetings from the Sevier County draft board arrived in camp on Nov. 10, sometime after the snowfall. The notice to appear before the board "within 48 hours" was delivered by Ernest Tipton, an assistant superintendent of the logging operation. Tipton rode a log train up the mountain so he could hand-deliver the message personally to Curtis, along with some farewell words.

Curtis already had his possessions "pretty well together" and soon set out walking down the railroad. He left it at the start of the Huskey Gap trail across Sugarland Mountain, and followed the trail as the nearest route to the home of his parents, Louis and Annie Newman McCarter in the Sugarlands.

His plans were to stay overnight, to leave his belongings and say good-bye before setting out early next morning on the walk down West Prong of Little Pigeon River to Sevierville. He did not expect he would be coming home again before the war ended.

But before he had traveled far, before he had walked through Gatlinburg, the word was spreading that the war had ended, at 11 o'clock (in Europe) on the morning of Nov. 11.

Like a rod and reel bring in a fish, the skidder hauled in logs on overhead cables from nearly a half-mile away. The cluster being uncoupled at lower left was one load. From top, Otis Bales was on the buggy; his brother Homer Bales in white shirt; Curtis McCarter; and Leander Parton. Picture was probably made with Amos Owenby's camera.

Curtis said there was no telephone anywhere in Gatlinburg in 1918, not even at the Mountain View Hotel completed several years before but at that time the only hotel in town. There was a telephone, though, at J. Rose Maples' store at Banner, beside the Banner Bridge that everybody crossed in travels between Pigeon Forge and Gatlinburg.

The draft board called Rose Maples and asked him to inform every young man, if he had the appearance of being on his way to report for military duty, that it would not now be necessary to report. The news spread almost as swiftly as if telephones had been more common, Curtis said.

Curtis gave himself a furlough after the good news that he would not have to go away to war. He loafed a few days before he returned to work at the skidder. "Your job will be waiting for you when you come back," Ernest Tipton had promised him. Ernest smiled when Curtis reclaimed the job after only a few days.

Curtis said the celebration of Thanksgiving Day was not as stylized in 1918 as it has since become. Still, people were aware of Thanksgiving, and the end of the war caused it to have special meaning that year.

Another memorable time for Curtis and Pearl McCarter was the day of their marriage, Feb. 29, the fifth Sunday in February, Leap Year, 1920. Mrs. McCarter was the daughter of Richard G. and Lydia Ogle, who owned a big part of the land that later became Cherokee Orchard and that is now inside the bounds of Great Smoky Mountains National Park.

What today would be considered a wealth of land did not protect its owners from having to work in that era, and Curtis and Pearl were soon headed to another logging job. They put a rope halter on the big white cow that would be their supplier of fresh milk. They walked her four miles across Sugarland Mountain and another four miles up Little River and Fish Camp Prong. Curtis would work there more than two years before they marched the cow back over the mountain, home again to the Sugarlands.

Curtis and Pearl McCarter in the yard of their Gatlinburg Home on Roaring Fork. The showy flowers were Mrs. McCarter's hobby, and they stopped hundreds of picture-taking tourists each season.

Curtis later became a frequent guide to botanists and biologists visiting the new national park for study of its plant and animal life. In teaching them the local, mountain names for plants, flowers, and trees, he pumped them for scientific names of the same plants. It was an exchange he continued to enjoy for the rest of his life.

The McCarters moved into downtown Gatlinburg in 1930 and Curtis was operating the riding stables full time by 1933, in partnership with Pearl's brother, Estel Ogle, at the beginning. At Curtis' death in 1982, the family still had the big frame home with its immaculate lawn, flowers, and shrubbery. They had kept it intact against dozens of offers, from people aware of its possibilities in a resort town that has very little land left to build on. The house has remained a place to come home to for a family of eight children and many grandchildren.

12

When Democrats became more plentiful

Democrats were so scarce in Sevier County at one time, Leonard Cogdill said, that there were ethnic jokes about Democrats.

"You boys work hard all week," Len's timber-cutting boss once told him, "and we'll go to Sevierville Saturday and see a Democrat."

He said there were only three registered Democrats in the town of Sevierville, and maybe none in the Smoky Mountain end of the county at the beginning of the 1930s.

There was a sudden upsurge in their numbers when Civilian Conservation Corps camps came to Sevier County in 1933. That was the beginning of the first term of President Franklin D. Roosevelt, a Democrat.

Any boy or man otherwise qualified could get into the CCC as a corpsman; the supervisory jobs were reserved for Democrats.

But there were so few Democrats in the mountain counties that Republicans, if they were quiet about it, were being given the jobs. Even the LEMs (local experienced men) who served as work leaders needed the sanction of one of Sevier County's Democratic Party officials to be appointed.

Len Cogdill and wife Dorothy Stinnett were married while Len was a LEM at the Sugarlands CCC camp above Gatlinburg. Dorothy was 16 years old and he was several years older.

Leonard and Dorothy Cogdill in the yard of their home near Dandridge, 1983.

Len already had worked for Little River Lumber Co. He was 16 years old when he started there as an axman, working beside his father, Leonard Cogdill Sr.

The older Cogdill was one of several of that family who became timber cutters of legendary skill. It was said of him that he could cut a lead notch so smooth that it looked like it had been sawed or planed.

Mattie Blair, Len Cogdill's mother, shortly before her death in 1914, when Len was two years old.

Young Len, learning from his father, also developed a skill that would guarantee him a job about anywhere timber was being cut.

"But I was never as good as my daddy. I couldn't hold him a light when he chopped," Len said.

Len's cousin Oscar Ogle went to West Virginia in 1935 to work in logging camps on Cherry River and Gauley River. Len Jr. and Sr. followed Oscar up there. They cut timber about 40 miles back in the mountains from where the sawmill was located.

They built a smoldering fire even on warm nights. They called it a "gnat smoke," because it was the only means they had of keeping the gnats away while they talked.

Bedbugs were another inevitable pest in the logging camps. "Kerosene was about all we had to fight bedbugs back then," Len said.

On his way home in 1936, Len stayed at a hotel in a big logging town before boarding a train for home the next day. He was tired of fighting the bedbugs and the gnats.

Of that last night in the hotel, he said, "I had to sleep in the middle of the floor. The bed was crawling with bedbugs."

When he returned he went to work with the Aluminum Company of America at Alcoa, tapping molten metal in the potrooms. The work was to his liking. He stayed more than 35 years before he retired.

It was also a life much more to Dorothy's liking. She was born at Elkmont at the peak of the logging boom. Her father, Willie Stinnett, was a timber-cutting contractor who moved often and took the family with him, from East Texas to East Tennessee. Dorothy studied in 17 different schools before she finished grade school.

Since then, she has liked the idea of being settled in one place.

13

If a lumberjack had wings

John Williams had the nickname of Rooster long before he wrecked a rickety airplane while trying to fly from what is now Elkmont Campground in the Smokies.

Williams was tall, muscular, and sometimes intimidating in physical appearance, and some of his friends were careful of what they said to him and when. This was notably true when Rooster was drinking, which is said to have been often.

But other friends regarded him as a generous "good ol' boy" who was exceptionally skillful at operating a log crane, to load timber onto rail cars.

It was through Knoxvillian Frank Andre that Rooster came to be interested in airplanes. Andre was 16 years old in 1922, the year he soloed as a pilot and began to make a living at flying. It was something he would continue to do for most of the rest of his life, through 25 years with Eastern Airlines and its forerunner, Pitcairn Aviation.

Andre was flying a Standard biplane, and sometimes a World War I surplus Jenny, in the first years. In his quest for adventure he was going places that the primitive, low-powered craft were not designed to go, across mountains that were higher than the plane's recommended ceiling.

He is believed to have landed a plane at Elkmont for the first time in 1923. That's where John Williams met him and talked with him about teaching him to fly.

Williams traveled to Knoxville for weekend instruction from Andre, at the pasture-turned-airfield on Sutherland Avenue. Sometimes he made the trip by train, through Little River Gorge and Townsend to the connection with Southern at Walland. Sometimes he drove his Star automobile through Fighting Creek Gap, Gatlinburg, Pigeon Forge and Sevierville.

Knoxvillian Ben Bower owned a quantity of Army surplus Jenny training planes he had bought at auction at the Army's Souther Field in Americus, Ga. Most were in wooden shipping crates and were sold, as is, for as little as $50, or as much as $500 if they were in new condition. The buyer did the assembling, which was to attach and guy the wings and install the OX-5 engine.

Andre family photo

Logger John Williams and Charles A. Lindbergh had in common that both bought World War I surplus Jenny training planes, like this one, from Knoxvillian Ben Bower. Pictured is Frank Andre, who gave Rooster flying fever and later was one of the pioneers who piloted Eastern Air Lines through its first 25 years.

– Photo from Dr. Frank E. Wilson

John "Rooster"" Williams, tall man at center, bought an airplane disassembled and had it shipped to Townsend by rail. The boy next to Williams was his son, Ben Mack Williams.

Andre later recalled that Rooster insisted on buying one and persuaded him to help put it together, including the stretching of Irish linen over the skeleton fuselage and wings.

Covering completed, the plane and detached wings were shipped from Knoxville to Townsend on two railroad flatcars, to be left on a siding there until Andre could make the trip to put the plane together. One of those who drove to Townsend with him was a Davenport Road neighbor, Frank E. Wilson, then a student at Knoxville High School and later a medical doctor, brigadier general in the U.S. Army, and national medical director of the American Red Cross for a time.

It was young Wilson's Kodak in someone else's hands that recorded the scene as the plane was rolled to a long level field a short distance up valley from Little River Lumber Co.'s band mill. The time was early 1925 and the pictures indicate late winter or early spring, before the trees put on leaves. Sometime soon afterward, Williams took leave from his job in the woods for

– **Photo from Dr. Frank E. Wilson**

The Jenny was rolled to its pasture landing field before the wings were attached. Young Frank E. Wilson from Knoxville rode the nose to balance it.

three days to fly paying passengers. Bob Farmer, then and later of Townsend, remembered the three days well.

"I was a teen-ager when he brought that plane in here," Bob said.

"John Rooster, we called him, had me selling tickets for him. He charged $3 a passenger and he'd land and take off in that field you're looking at." Bob motioned to a meadow across the road from the home he and his wife Ruby built in the heart of Tuckaleechee Cove.

"Between taking in money I'd walk down to the Townsend Mercantile Co. to the only gasoline pump in town. I hauled him his gas five-gallon at a time, pulling it in my wagon.

"He took me for a ride, my first airplane ride, and that was my pay for helping him. I still remember how scared I was, but it wasn't because I didn't trust Rooster. I didn't have anybody to compare him with as an airplane pilot.

"There wasn't a windsock here, but he didn't seem to care which way the wind blew. He'd land and take off in whichever direction was handiest. He hauled a lot of people and made some money, but he needed to get back to his job on the log loader if he was to keep it."

Bob said Rooster wanted to take the plane to Elkmont, but wasn't sure he was ready yet to fly it into that valley between high mountains. Again he called on Frank Andre to come up from Knoxville to help him.

"Now fly it to Elkmont for me, so I can work on it next winter," Williams said when Andre arrived.

Remembering all that in the 1950s, Andre said he had been braced for Rooster's request. "He was not easy to say 'no' to," Andre recalled. He did agree to fly the Jenny to Elkmont, but exacted a promise that he would not be asked to fly it out again.

Paul Henry said it had been announced beforehand that Frank and Rooster would be flying in on that certain day, and that a crowd gathered apprehensively. The crowd cheered and whistled when the plane landed safely on the Elkmont island that is no longer an island, but today is part of the largest campground in Great Smoky Mountains National Park. They landed in the area of a dirt automobile racetrack upstream from where a church stood, where Andre had set down on previous visits with other planes.

Frank's parting advice was that Rooster not try to take off from there before putting more dope on the linen covering to make it more taut over the airframe, and waterproof. But there was a certain feeling among those who knew John Williams well that he would try to fly his airplane at the first opportunity, perhaps on the next Sunday, when nobody worked in the woods.

In that expectancy a crowd gathered to watch what would soon become John Williams' first and last flight from Elkmont. Rooster's wife Maude and their son Ben Mack, then about 13 years old, arrived early.

Maude said that when Frank Andre gave him flying lessons it excited him more than anything she had seen happen to him. And now that he was in the cockpit at the end of the takeoff strip, she was braced for the worst but hoping for the best. She knew he had been drinking that morning.

Close acquaintances have said it was a mystery how Rooster was able to afford an airplane, flying lessons, and an automobile on a logger's pay, although his skill at operating machinery made him one of the better paid.

One of his Elkmont neighbors of the Prohibition era said he made whisky with a wink from one of the company's higher managers. The neighbor kept her copper double boiler hanging on the porch between washdays, and knew when it was missing from its nail that Rooster was using it to make another run.

At least two of the men who worked with Williams on the loading crew during the week went along to the island to help start the airplane's engine. This was done by one of them "pulling through" on the wooden propeller. Rooster sat in the cockpit and nursed the throttle, choke and ignition controls.

The OX-5, liquid-cooled eight-cylinder, 90-horsepower engine did start, and that's when Walter Cole came on the scene. Fifty years later Walter remembered it this way:

"I lived on Jakes Creek and I walked down there to the island. Just a little old strip they had to land on and take off.

"John was in the plane and he was running the motor. I walked close to the plane and I asked him, 'Can I go with you?'

"But he said, 'I ain't never took this thing up from this place, and I don't want you with me.' Then he said to me, 'Kick the scotches out.'"

So Walter kicked away the rocks that were put in front of and behind both landing wheels to "scotch" them and keep the plane from rolling. Two of Williams' friends meanwhile held a long fence rail against the landing gear, above the wheels, to hold the plane back while he revved the engine.

At Rooster's signal they quickly withdrew the rail, and now he was bouncing downfield, downriver, in the direction of Cove Mountain, heading for the open place beside the church, hoping to be airborne in time to clear the big boulder at the end of the takeoff strip.

He did get the plane off the ground but didn't clear the rock. Walter said one wingtip grazed it, and the Jenny came to rest leaning on its nose and one crippled wing.

"It wasn't hurt much. Just one wing and the propeller," Walter said. "I went down there and he unbuckled and got out. He wasn't hurt — nothing except his pride."

Maude said all she could see at first was the dust the plane raised when it wrecked. She remembered crying.

Then a woman from one of the families that summered at Elkmont came over and told her Rooster did not appear to be hurt. Maude said later it wasn't true—a story told about her for years—that she ran to the plane and gave him an angry scolding. She did go to him, she said, but was too "choked up" to say anything.

Ben T. Thomas was eight years old. He was at Elkmont for the summer with his parents, E.L. and Margaret Thomas of Knoxville. Ben saw the takeoff from his perch on a boulder near the starting point. He ran to the wreck scene and salvaged one of the bigger slivers of the shattered propeller.

– Photo by Vic Weals Jr.

Ben T. Thomas cherished a souvenir sliver of propeller more than 50 years after Rooster's airplane was stopped by the boulder behind Ben, now in Elkmont Campground.

He kept it for years at the family's Elkmont cottage, where he later lived in retirement. It was lost or mislaid for a time, and the way Ben found it was that a family member came up with it as a likely stick of firewood. It was saved from that fate and fastened to the cottage wall, in hope that it wouldn't again be mistaken for anything trivial.

Jess Cole said the plane stood there so long that bees stored honey in the comb of the radiator. He said Rooster dismounted the engine and laid it on the porch of his home at Elkmont, until finally he took it to a garage in Sevierville. Word got around that he had installed the engine in an automobile and planned to race it. "How fast will it go?" Jess asked him.

"Faster than the word of God," Rooster said.

Bob Farmer remembered a car wreck Williams had sometime after his airplane mishap. "She'd fly if she had wings," Rooster said to a companion

70

before his car left the road and soared into Short Creek, near the later site of Wilson's Restaurant at the lower end of Tuckaleechee Cove.

Maude said it left him crippled awhile, and she had him taken to their home at Elkmont where she could look after him until he recovered. Sometime later Williams left East Tennessee to run a log loader on a ponderosa pine sawmilling operation, in the mountains of southern New Mexico near Alamogordo. He met a woman there and later mailed Maude some papers for a divorce that he said he had been granted from her, Maude, in old Mexico.

Still later, sometime in the 1930s, he wrote to Maude again and told her he was coming home. He said he was lonesome for his family, meaning her and their son, Ben Mack, who by now was married and had started his own family.

But Rooster never did see home again. His new wife shot and killed him.

Maude tried to have his body sent back here for reburial. She gave up on that finally because it was difficult to arrange from a distance. She journeyed to New Mexico to within 100 miles of Alamogordo. She said she at first intended to go all the way and visit his grave there, but decided against that, too, finally.

Blind and infirm in her final years, Maude had compassionate care and a home in Knoxville with her daughter-in-law, Lena Williams. Maude died at the age of 93 in November 1988.

– Williams family photo
Maude Williams (from left), her husband John and John's mother Florence were at Elkmont about 10 years before he learned to fly.

John Williams leans from the cab at left as he plies his main job of running an American log loader. The men on the log were there only for the picture, and not because their work required it. It was dangerous to ride a dangling log.

14

Hobe knew horses

Carl Abbott was a boy helping his father drive cattle to Thunderhead Prong when he first saw the clearing known as the "Blowdown." Carl's father, Perry Abbott, told him it was a storm sometime before 1900 that flattened several acres of timber and gave the place its name.

The wind left one great yellow poplar tree standing almost alone, with all but one of its upper limbs blown away. The limb extended from the top of the tree like the handle of a giant walkingstick.

Raymer Brackin was in the crew that cut the tree in the 1930s, and had these memories of it more than 50 years later.

The huge main trunk yielded three logs, each 16 feet long, and the limb that formed the walkingstick "handle" made another 16-foot log about two feet thick.

Ashley Moore standing beside it gives an idea of the girth of the "Walkingstick" poplar at the Blowdown, a cove on Thunderhead Prong of the Middle Fork of Little River. Moore was the grandson of William M. Walker, the first settler of Middle Prong.

Luke Lawson of Cades Cove worked a team on Hazel Creek, on the North Carolina slope of the Smokies, about 1915. Lawson was killed three years later in the fighting in World War I.

Brackin remembered the diameter of the "butt cut," or first log, as being "nearly eight feet." An eight-foot saw did the cutting, with one of the handles removed so the saw could be pulled through the thickest part.

Brackin and brother-in-law John Ownby did the sawing. Luther McCarter was the crew's chipper, but didn't use his ax that day. The lead notch was cut with a saw by Ownby and Brackin.

With few upper branches in its own crown and no smaller timber nearby to cushion its fall, the Walkingstick hit the ground very hard, but didn't shatter, Brackin said.

The richest acre logged by the Little River Lumber Co. was in that neighborhood, between Shut-In Prong and Lost Cove on Sams Creek, with 100,000 board feet measure of timber cut from it. "There were trees in there as big as anywhere, five and six feet through," Brackin said.

"Sams Creek was a pretty place before they put the incline-railroad in there," Carl Abbott said. Shut-In Creek gets its name from being very difficult to enter above its mouth, Carl said. It heads up at about 4,200 feet of elevation and cascades steeply to where it enters Thunderhead Prong at 2,100 feet above sea level.

Hobart Hayes helped haul the Walkingstick logs. It was near there that he saw another poplar log so thick that when it rolled off the slope and landed on end on the railroad, it stood on end there until it was lifted to a flatcar.

"I've hauled some good ones," Hayes said. "I hauled one poplar from Lynn Camp Prong in above Tremont that had six cuts, counting the logs from the limbs. The butt cut was hollow. It was 11 feet across one way and 11 feet 11 inches another way. The whole tree averaged 3,000 (board) feet to the cut." The cuts Hayes described were all logs 16 feet long.

The hollow stump was left with high walls, and a roof built over it and a doorway cut to make a roomy cowshed.

Hobe Hayes drove a team of logging horses for eight years on Middle Prong and its branches. He and his wife Betty Owenby Hayes lived in four portable houses set end-to-end, and all four of their children were born there. As the timber cutters cut out and moved farther up the valley, the houses moved with them, two to a railroad flatcar. A log crane picked them up and set them off again, on foundations already built.

Hobe reminisced in March of 1989, shortly before his death at the age of 87. His wife died in 1976.

He started with the lumber company in 1917 at the age of 15, on Fish Camp Prong above Elkmont. He worked for the "original wood hicks," he said. They liked him and called him "The Kid," and gave him his first dip of snuff.

His first job was to dip water from the branch and throw it on the pole road. The poles were beech and birch when those were available, and if the poles were kept wet, a trail of logs would slide over them like they were roller-bearings.

Hobe already knew something about horses, and the wood hicks taught him more. Some of them were drifters whose skill at handling horses was almost a guarantee of a job when they moved to another lumber company. They tried to save a dollar or more for every day they worked, for a grubstake between jobs, and some declined to stay longer than 90 days with the same employer. There was a superstition that most men killed in the very dangerous work of logging were men who stayed on the same job too long. Joe Carver quoted a saying some of them had:

"Ninety days, 90 dollars, and a hundred days a dead man."

Hobart Hayes didn't drift, and drove the same team for eight years in his final job on Middle Prong. The

Hobart Hayes in 1989, on the day he reminisced on his life as a logger on Little River a half-century earlier.

horses were Harry and Brownie, weight 1,680 pounds each, so gentle that he took his very young children for rides on them on Sundays, the only day that there was no work in the woods.

Ralph, the second Hayes son, was asking his mother for brown sugar to feed the horses about as soon as he was allowed to be outdoors unsupervised. "The horses would follow little Ralph, wanting more sugar, and people got a kick out of that," Raymer Brackin said.

Hobe got up about 4 a.m. in summer. He fed the horses oats and timothy hay, which he ordered up from Townsend by the rail carload. He packed their lunch in sacks tied to their hames, a gallon of feed for each horse. At feeding time he'd try to find a hollow log that could be split to make a trough.

When he came in at night, before he did anything for himself, he'd drive Harry and Brownie into the creek to wash the mud off, being specially careful to clean the caked mud and gravel from their hooves. Hardened mud in a hoof brought on an infection which the teamsters called the "thrush" or the "evil foot." There was no cure for the evil foot, and in time it would cause the hoof to fall off. That crippled the animal and caused it great pain, so that it had to be destroyed by being shot.

Hobart Hayes and three of his children, Clyde, Gladys, and Ralph, with the horse, Harry, at the Little River Lumber Co. work camp at the Blowdown. The youngest child, now Dorothy Ingle, wasn't in the picture because she wasn't born until 1938, the Hayes family's final year at Tremont. Gladys is now Mrs. Crum Harper, of Rockford.

Very hot days endangered the horses. "You'd stand them in the shade. You couldn't work them after they got real hot," Hobe said. The flies that swarmed in the fall would make the horses' legs bleed, and the only insect spray available didn't keep them away long.

Tiny, almost invisible gnats were the plague for humans. "The gnats come nigh eating us up," Hobe said. "Rub a little coal oil on you and it kept them off awhile. If a gnat was as big as a rattlesnake it would have killed you in a minute."

As the loggers advanced up Thunderhead Prong with railroad, cable skidders, and log cranes, the horses were being taken into places that had been wilderness since the beginning of forests on these mountains. It was in those places that the teamsters learned that horses had a natural fear of the black bear and the rattlesnake. Hobe said he and Aaron Ownby killed 11 rattlesnakes in one day, "on Sams Creek in the first hollow to the left," and it was the horses that first sensed their presence.

Hobe said that 21 logs were the most he ever hauled behind his horses in one trail. He figured on two trails a day down the long hollow, and sometimes rode the header log. "You'd pick a heavy header log, maybe three or four feet in diameter, one that would ride level. My boy Ralph rode with me sometimes," he said

Ramps, a wild, onionlike vegetable not listed in the smaller dictionaries, grew abundantly in the higher hollows visited by the teamsters, and were an early spring treat to many families after a winter of nothing green to eat. Ashley Perryman, the teamster foreman with whom Hobart Hayes worked on Little River, let his men off work early when they came across a ramp patch, so they could gather a "mess" to take home. It was always a "mess of ramps" they enjoyed, traditionally eaten with side meat (bacon), cornbread, and pinto beans. Or sometimes they were eaten with eggs, or raw like green onions.

Ashley Perryman was 93 years old in 1990 and still enjoying a ritual spring feast of ramps, usually at the home of friends who shared his fondness for them. Because of the pervasive aroma they would have left in dining room and kitchen, a smell that offends many people not accultured to ramps, they weren't served at the retirement home where Ashley lived in Sevierville.

Hobart Hayes said he generally enjoyed the years on what he called "the Tremont job," and his wife liked them because he came straight home from work every evening. His pay was $82 a month, and no charge for the portable set of houses his family lived in. Betty Hayes fed two boarders at $5 a week each, a big part of which was profit because of the low cost of provisions in the 1930s. The Hayes family saved money, and when they left they were able to buy five acres and build a house on it at Oak View, north of Chilhowee Mountain on Ellejoy Creek.

He worried whether he'd ever again find work that he enjoyed as much as logging and caring for the horses. He remembered a day when Brownie fell while headed up the trail. The horse stayed down awhile, as though he wondered whether he was hurt too much to get to his feet. Hobe reassured him, "You're all right, Brownie. Get up." And Brownie did.

Hobe Hayes helped take up the rails when the lumber company left Middle Prong in 1938, and surrendered the land stripped of its timber to the new national park. After some layoff, he was hired by the Aluminum Company to operate a crane in the blacksmith shop at Alcoa. It turned out to be something he liked doing, and he stayed 27 years until he retired.

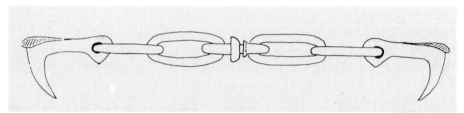

Elbert Wilkey's drawing (above) of a pair of grabs as the points would be positioned for driving into two logs, to connect them in a trail. Lonas Clark (below)holds the real thing. Grabs enough to tie a long trail weighed several hundred pounds. It was the job of the grabjack to drive the points into the logs, and to knock them free again at the end of the trail. Dragging the grabs back up the trail behind the horses was one of the nuisances of team logging.

15

Little River a long thread in lives of Martha and Raymer

The older children of Martha and Raymer Brackin started school at Townsend, riding a bus from Tremont every day. But the family soon moved away from logging, and all five Brackin children graduated from Blount County's Porter High School.

And all five studied past high school, one to graduate from the University of Tennessee in electrical engineering, one as a registered nurse from Knoxville General Hospital, and the other three from medical, technical and business training.

Martha and Raymer met when they were children in school in a little portable building on Fish Camp Prong, a remote tributary of Little River above Elkmont. Both were from families employed by the lumber company.

Martha's parents were Ellen Dodgen Ownby and Pinkney Ownby, distinguished from other Pink Ownbys by the name of "timber-cutting Pink." Raymer says of his father-in-law that he "was every inch a sawyer," one of the more skillful in an age of talented saw crews.

Pink's son John Ownby also became a sawyer for part of his working life. But there were so many named John Ownby, several of them timber cutters, that it wouldn't have helped much to call any one of them "timber-cutting John."

John and Raymer worked at opposite ends of a crosscut saw through what Raymer remembers as his most productive years as a lumberjack.

"If you had a sharp saw and a good buddy at the other end of it, that was about as much fun as playing a fiddle," Raymer says. "But if you had a bad working buddy, one who didn't know what he was doing, he could get you killed in a minute."

"We'd start the day carrying one saw—a six-foot saw most days. If it was big poplars to be cut, we might take an eight-foot saw. But the longer the saw was, the harder it was to carry through the woods," Raymer says.

He says a saw crew could cut a tree thicker than the saw was long. They did that by removing the handle from one end of the saw, and letting one man pull it through the thickest part of the log.

Raymer started with the lumber company as flagman on a skidder in 1920, before he was 12 years old. He was only 30 years old when he left, in 1939. His working years since then have been with the Aluminum Company of America at Alcoa.

In retirement Martha and Raymer live at Townsend on Little River. It's the same stream that plunged and roared through their adventurous years higher in the Smokies. Now it eddies clear and peaceful through the flatter channel past their back yard.

– Photo by Vic Weals

Hands once calloused from cutting timber now knit coverlets and piece intricate quilts. Martha and Raymer Brackin share the hobby, which she taught him early in his retirement from the aluminum plants at Alcoa, Tenn.

16

Hotel for hearty eaters

Bernice and Ernest Headrick were managing the new Tremont Hotel in the summer of 1926, and Bernice's sister, Eula Fox, was soon on her way from Waldens Creek to work for the Headricks. Eula was 17 and would be a junior at Sevier County High School that fall.

The lumber company built the two-story hotel mostly as a place to feed and house employees who didn't have their families with them, and the Headricks tried to serve the kind of food that satisfied hearty eaters. Ernest had cooked in hotels and restaurants in Chicago, and Bernice's artistry in the kitchen had earned the praise of discriminating appetites on Waldens Creek.

The Tremont Hotel as it looked soon after the Little River Lumber Co. opened it on Midle Prong in 1926. The dam in center foreground diverted water to a wheel and generator to provide electric light.

The hotel was on Lynn Camp Prong just above where it joins Thunderhead Prong to form Middle Prong of Little River. The most practical way to reach Tremont was to walk up the railroad from the Forks above Townsend, or to hitch a ride on a train of empty log cars. Roy M. Myers was conductor-brakeman the day Eula was in need of a ride, and he motioned her to an open flatcar.

The roadbed of the former railroad up Lynn Camp Prong, above Tremont, was a hiking trail enjoyed by Joe Murphy Jr. of Knoxville in April of 1990.

When they reached the Wildcat Bluff, across the river from Spruce Flats Branch, Roy came to Eula and told her that was as far as the rod engine would be going. A Shay engine would pull the empties up the steeper grades ahead. Young Shirley Broome was engineer of the Shay, and Roy pointed him out. "You're going to like Shirley Broome," he told Eula. In less than another four years they would be married.

Meanwhile, Eula alternated at finishing high school, working at Tremont, and teaching at Midway and Alder Branch on a high school certificate. After her marriage to Shirley, she taught all subjects in the school at Tremont. Their only child, the daughter they also named Shirley, was born at Tremont.

"We fondly remember Tremont as a very civil place," Eula said at a 1990 reunion that drew several dozen of her former students.

The hotel was gone in 1990, except for a portion of poured concrete foundation. Still visible was the race that once led water to a wheel to turn a generator, to provide lights for the hotel, school, company store, doctor's office, and machine shop.

In fall, a man was hired full time to clean falling leaves away from the mill wheel. There was no reserve source of power, and the lights went out suddenly if leaves blocked water from turning the wheel.

The Tremont Hotel was not an elegant establishment, but it is a pleasant place in the memory of those who knew it. Loggers occupied the ground level, where their calked boots tattooed the rough-sawed heavy pine flooring. Transients were assigned to the second floor.

Gnats were the memorial unpleasantness of life at Tremont, Eula Broome said, "so small you could hardly see them, yet they'd bite like fury.

You had to build gnat smokes to try to keep them away. You had to spray. It was almost impossible to stay outside at night."

After the Little River Lumber Co. folded its Middle Prong operations late in the 1930s, and yielded its cut-over lands to Great Smoky Mountains National Park, Eula continued teaching and Shirley kept at railroading. He and John Compton drove diesel locomotives for L&N in the wartime building of Oak Ridge, and they later worked for Smoky Mountain Railroad, hauling materials for the construction of Douglas Dam.

Shirley's untimely death at the age of 50 in 1953 was from natural causes and not from railroading. He had survived uninjured in several mishaps, including the wreck of his runaway train on Marks Creek in 1931. Shirley had been too young to remember the death of his father in 1906. Rubin Broome was killed as a logger for the Tellico River Lumber Co., when a log rolled over him on Bald River.

A log train downbound from Elkmont to Townsend travels the grade that was quickly converted to an automobile road beginning late in 1925. The locomotive is the Baldwin Mallet, No. 148.

17

Kates Ogle and the dynamite express

L ittle River Lumber Co. began removing the rails up East Prong late in 1925, but did not forewarn the families who had summer cottages at Elkmont. The company was afraid they'd try to keep the trains running by court order, if they had advance notice that the rails would be taken up.

Brazil Patty Cromwell remembered it that way 65 years later, at her Townsend home in June of 1990. Brazil worked in the lumber company's office at Townsend in 1925, and answered some of the angry telephone calls that followed the railroad's dismantling. Flo Dew was railroad superintendent.

The line from Townsend to Elkmont was profitable in the 16 years it hauled both logs and people. But now that the timber had been cut in the entire watershed of East Prong, most of the passenger traffic would be on weekends to and from the privately-owned cottages around the Wonderland Hotel and Appalachian Club .

KATES OGLE

W.B. Townsend, the lumber company president, did not intend to furnish transportation indefinitely and at a loss, Brazil said. He hoped to avoid a court fight by taking up the rails swiftly beginning at the Elkmont end, and loading them on flatcars behind No. 105. Some of the rails were taken immediately to Middle Prong, where the company was laying track toward the new Tremont logging camp.

Most of the cottage owners were from Knoxville, and at the beginning of the colony they came all the way from Knoxville by train. In the 1920s, when more dependable automobiles became available and a decent motor roadway was built up Little River as far as Townsend, they drove that far in their

85

The Long Arm, a rocky spine that descends at left from Meigs Mountain, was blasted and notched here in 1907 to make a path for the Little River Lumber Company's railroad from Townsend. No. 105 was posed in the Long Arm Cut in 1909, soon after the Townsend-Elkmont railroad was completed.

automobiles, usually on Friday evening or Saturday morning. As long as the railroad ran up East Prong, there was no room in the narrow gorge for a motor road too. So the commuters depended on the daily passenger train to take them from Townsend to Elkmont.

The two views, made 77 years apart, have about the same camera angle. Conversion from railroad to automobile road, of loose gravel in the beginning, was begun in 1926. The mountain rising steeply in the background is Cove Mountain.

The road from Gatlinburg through Fighting Creek Gap to Elkmont was not an attractive alternative well into the 1920s, because of its long, steep grade that could burn out clutches and brakes in one trip. Several Maryville College students were killed on the hill when the brakes of their truck failed.

Kates Ogle, from Banner below Gatlinburg, was 16 years old when he drove a Model T Ford pickup truck to help build a new road that would replace the Elkmont-Townsend railroad. The job started in 1926 after the last rails had been removed, and the speed with which it was started may have owed something to the fact that the family of Tennessee Gov. Austin Peay had a cottage at Elkmont.

The former railroad right of way was narrow for a motor road, but the gentle grade designed for rod locomotives was excellent for automobile travel. The roadbuilders were taking up the crossties and covering the roadbed with gravel from a rock crusher located just above the Long Arm. Kates said it was a very coarse limestone gravel.

The men who worked around the noisy, steam-powered crusher called it a "rattlebox," and the creek branch that tumbles into Little River there is still called Rattlebox Branch. Nobody lived on Rattlebox Branch, and that left the road crews feeling safe to drink its water. Kates, a farmer, fox hunter, and mountain man all his long life, wouldn't drink from a stream that was inhabited on its upper reaches.

The Metcalf family farther down the gorge showed their appreciation for the road by bringing the workmen cold water from a spring. "They brought it in a bucket with a dipper standing in it, and we all drank from that dipper," Kates said. The thoughtfulness of the Metcalfs was remembered when the National Park Service put their name on the Metcalf Bottoms Picnic Area. "They raised the prettiest corn and beans there you ever saw," Kates said.

His duties as driver of the pickup were to haul gasoline to the air compressors, and to haul dynamite from Maryville and Townsend. Diesel engines weren't as universal in construction work as they would later be, and gasoline engines powered the air compressors. The air was for pneumatic drilling of holes into rock, for placing of dynamite charges to widen the right of way.

The little truck was stout enough to haul one drum (50 to 60 gallons) of gasoline at a time. That was quite a load, and the truck was equipped with an extra-low gear to handle it. It was like "driving a bomb" to haul gasoline over that rough, unfinished road, Kates said. But it was the dynamite cargoes, 18 to 24 cases, 36 sticks to the case, that made him most uneasy.

Kates Ogle and Mamie Watson were married in 1930, and one of their favorite pastimes 50 years later was to drive their new, air-conditioned pickup truck to the Long Arm Cut. They'd park in one of the pull-off places and walk up and down the road, looking at scenes that are never tiresome: Little River tumbling green and clean down its rocky gorge, Cove Mountain to the north rising more than 1,600 feet in one sweep.

The road today is much wider and smoother than the rough gravel trail they put down in 1926, and a wide, steel bridge replaces the converted railroad trestle that carried automobile traffic in the beginning. "I'm proud of what we did here," Kates Ogle said.

18

Light at the end of logging

W T. Cope moved to Elkmont in Sevier County, Tenn., in the Great Smoky Mountains, in 1910 to keep books for Little River Lumber Co. One of his sons, Frederick Arnold Cope, then 16, took a job driving a team of horses, snaking logs out of the hollows down a pole road to the railroad.

Young Cope took his rest periods with the horses where he could watch the steam-powered skidders, fascinated as they lifted clusters of logs from the slopes and hollows, carrying them suspended on overhead cables nearly a half-mile to landings beside the railroad sidings.

To operate a skidder was something he knew he'd like to do, and he had in mind to try it sometime. But in 1911 W. T. Cope moved his family to a home on Euclid Avenue in Knoxville, where he thought his sons might have easier and safer employment opportunities. Fred slipped through the back bedroom window a week later and walked most or all of the way to Elkmont, probably 50 miles.

The Smokies were home to him by now and he was determined to stay there. It was several months before the family learned for certain where he was. The other Copes meanwhile moved back to Gaston County, N.C., and left young Fred to pursue the life of a logger.

He worked now as a fireman, shoveling coal to the boiler of a Shay

Fred and Dora Cope on their wedding day. She was 16 years old.

locomotive on Fish Camp Prong above Elkmont. He boarded with the family of Robert V. Woodruff, a railroad foreman for the lumber company.

In 1915, at the age of 20, Fred married the Woodruffs' daughter, Dora. Soon thereafter he was promoted to engineer of skidder No. 1. Thus he began a lengthy career that would take him and Dora into most of the main and branch hollows of the Little River watershed.

The skidder was hauled and relocated from Fish Camp to Three Forks, Peawood Hollow, Higdon Camp, Jakes Creek, Wildcat Flats, Stringtown, and Marks Cove. Dave Grey, Commodore Gilland, and Alex Cole worked with him for some or most of the years.

Fred's children remember him saying that Peawood Hollow in 1916 and

Crew of No. 1 skidder (from left): foreman Fred Cope, Dave Grey, and Commodore Gilland. Wheelbarrow was for hauling firewood to the boiler.

1917 was the most difficult place. The mountain was so steep there that moving the heavy skidder in and setting it up to operate safely was an exasperating beginning. So treacherous was the footing that only one set of portable living quarters could be installed. Fred, Dora and their infant daughter Wilma lived in the quarters, and four of the loggers lived in a lean-to at the back and ate at the Cope table. The others came up on the train each morning and rode it back to the bigger camp below at night.

A steam log crane wrecked one day a few feet from the Cope house, tumbling into the ravine below with the log it was hoisting. Dora took the baby and ran up the tracks away from the hiss of escaping steam, afraid the boiler might explode. It was in Peawood Hollow that the Cope cow stumbled out of her steep pasture and broke her neck and died.

When rumors flourished that Little River Lumber Co. would sell its holdings to be included in the new Great Smoky Mountains National Park, Fred began to worry again about employment. Logging was most of what he knew, and it, as a steady livelihood, was fading throughout the Southern mountains. The coming industrial work opportunity appeared to him to be in the generation and transmission of electricity.

Fred saw a magazine advertisement for a correspondence course, in which a Chicago school promised to teach its students by mail how to build a generator to produce electric current for lights.

The lessons began arriving and Fred's nights were spent studying. Some of the math problems were more complex than nine grades of school had prepared him for. When he needed help he took his questions to Milas Ownby, a bookkeeper for the lumber company. Ownby helped him patiently until his problems were solved and understood.

The final lesson required him to build a generator with the parts, including the wire and two light bulbs, mailed to him in a box. He built the generator and then built a trough to carry water from the creek to a wheel which would turn it and make electricity.

The school overlooked one vital piece—a drive belt to turn the generator. Dora made a belt from a strip of denim cloth. Fred ran wires to the kitchen and sitting room, where he hung the bulbs and sockets from the ceiling. Everything ready, he went outside to the master switch and turned it on, and the room was suddenly lit several times brighter than it had been by kerosene lamp only seconds before. Electricity had come to Stringtown logging camp.

When the Copes left Stringtown for another site in 1927, Fred sold his generating outfit to Creed Spurgeon, who moved it to Pittman Center on Webbs Creek east of Gatlinburg.

It was in the same period that the Copes owned the first radio in camp. Dora remembered neighbors gathering in the yard to listen to election returns.

Five of the 10 Cope children were born in Little River work camps, and some of the older ones were married and gone from home before the last

Fred and Dora Cope and their first child, daughter Wilma, stood for a picture in Peawood Hollow in 1917, where they lived in a portable house near his job as engineer of Little River Lumber Co.'s skidder No. 1.

were born. Dora's child-bearing years extended from 1915, when she was 17, to 1941, when she was 43.

The Copes were concerned that their children be educated. In the years on Middle Prong and its tributaries, Fred sat at the big kitchen table with them many nights to help and prod them in their homework. There were books and newspapers to read even when other material possessions were scarce.

The family grew in prosperity after its logging camp years, and some of the younger children went on to college.

Cope first left Little River in 1930 to build a high tension line from Waterville, N.C., to Knoxville for Tennessee Public Service Co. The steel A-frame towers his crew erected were still in service after a half-century, and could be seen in Dutch Valley at the Knoxville end.

He left logging again in 1937 to be foreman of crews that strung lines in Sevier, Blount, Union, Grainger, Loudon and Knox counties. When the former privately owned power company was succeeded by Knoxville Utilities Board, to distribute electricity generated by the new Tennessee Valley Authority, he was still there along with some of his former skidder crew-mates. Climbing tall trees to rig log-hauling cables was very much like scaling steel towers to string electric lines. Many of the engineering problems were the same.

Fred Cope was immensely satisfied to be able to bring electricity to rural families who had never known its wonderful convenience. When "Cope's

A 1915 gathering of logging camp neighbors high above Elkmont included five of their hounds, some of them bear dogs. Fred Cope, Jim Grey, Dave Grey, Jim Wilson, Noah Watson, R.V. Woodruff, Luther Woodruff and Jim Headrick were among those present.

gang" had finished all long lines in Union and Grainger counties, Fred had this to say:

"Many times when we worked close to a country school the children would gather at the windows and doors to see our performance. I have often asked teachers to dismiss their classes so the students could see the men do the work which would bring the long-wanted electricity to their homes and neighborhood.

Before they became brothers-in-law, Luther Woodruff (left) and Fred Cope were friends who worked together on Little River and hunted together, mostly for wild turkey, squirrel, and raccoon. Fred's dog, Jack, at right beside him, was at least partly of a bear-hunting breed, but a sensitive animal. After a move from Three Forks to Eldorado, Fred scolded Jack for eating feed intended for the hogs. Jack then sulked back to the old home at Three Forks, under Clingmans Dome.

"At last our job is finished, with new friends and acquaintances added along the way. The 'light men,' as we are called, will long be remembered by the children in the country schools."

Fred A. Cope pointed his camera mostly at friends and relatives, and at the same time produced pictures that were often technically excellent. Cope was behind the camera here; his subjects on horseback were Jim Headrick and Luther Woodruff. Between the horses at front was Cope's father-in-law, railroad foreman Robert V. Woodruff. The horses ranged to 2,000 pounds each in weight.

19

The Wonderland Hotel

Dr. C.E. Brehm, front, wrote many of his speeches in the quiet of the Wonderland Hotel's screened annex. Brehm was president of the University of Tennessee from 1947 to 1959. Others in the picture on the hotel steps were members of the Brehm family, wife Ruth at left, daughter Alice Jean Brehm Williamson in rear, son J. Fred Brehm at right, Fred's daughter Donna beside her grandmother, and a Brehm cousin, Marian Dapp, at center.

The Wonderland's long porch, rocking chairs, and ceiling fans took its guests back in time.

Rear of the Wonderland Hotel at Elkmont in 1989. After two more summer seasons, it was scheduled to be dismantled.

20

A hollow tree for a cowbarn

Loggers who had their families in camp might keep a cow or two as an only source of fresh milk and butter. Neither product was sold at the commissaries of Little River Lumber Co., for lack of refrigeration and for other reasons. Evaporated or condensed brands were available, but most people accustomed to milk fresh from the cow did not like the taste of the canned versions.

Lou and John Foster kept two cows at their place about seven miles above Elkmont and near Three Forks. Having two gave them a better chance that one would "come fresh" when the other was about to "go dry."

Harvey and Mary Click sometimes kept two cows in camp, to feed a family that eventually included 12 children.

John and two of their three sons worked for the lumber company in that period, right after World War I, in jobs that required them to leave home very early each morning and not return until 12 or more hours later. Too, John W. Swaggerty says, it was custom in the Smokies, up to that time and later, for women to do the milking. For those reasons and possibly others, milking the cows and feeding them was left mostly to Lou.

John and Lou Foster kept cows at their place near Three Forks, on Little River above Elkmont.

The cows roamed the woods daytimes, munching at whatever tufts of green they could find where the timber cutters had already cleared. Owners of cows were expected to keep them away from areas where the saw and ax crews were currently working.

The cows sometimes ranged so far they could not easily be rounded up at milking time, although the prospect of an evening meal of grain usually lured them home. Hay and grain could be ordered from the branch commissary at Elkmont.

Most families penned their cows overnight and turned them back to the woods after the morning milking. Cow barns were built by the cow owners and ranged in sophistication from a frame shed to a bark-covered lean-to. A roof was built over the hollow stump of a giant poplar above Tremont, to make a cow a roundhouse about 11 feet across.

While the Fosters lived in a board-and-batten house built at the site, most of the families lived in what were called "cars" or "set-off houses." They earned the latter name because they were moved to new locations on railroad flatcars and lifted off by a log crane. Several units could be joined end-to-end to accommodate more people, and they amounted to a primitive version of today's mobile home.

Cows were sometimes taken inside the little homes on moving day, and there are stories of cows being milked while the train climbed slowly to a new camp farther up the mountain valley.

Duvall family photo

Crane is about to set off one little portable house next to another as the quarters of a logger's family on Citico Creek, next door to the Smokies. Canvas side curtains on the crane were to protect the operator from the cold, as much as he could be protected.

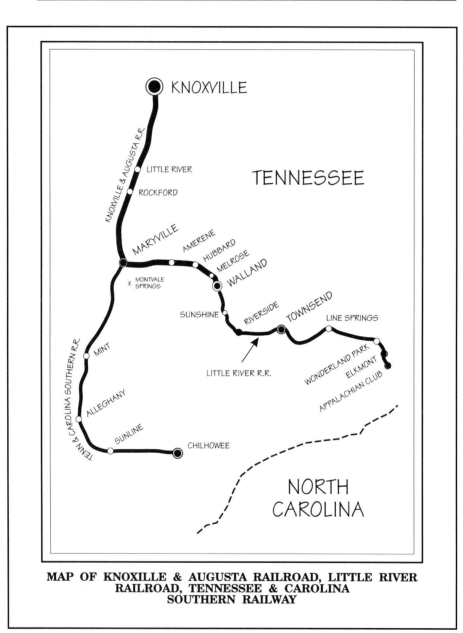

MAP OF KNOXILLE & AUGUSTA RAILROAD, LITTLE RIVER RAILROAD, TENNESSEE & CAROLINA SOUTHERN RAILWAY

Daily trains left Knoxville's Southern station at 7:30 a.m. in 1915 to arrive at Elkmont three hours later. The trains brought ice cream and other perishables before they were available in places without railroad service. The Tennessee & Carolina Southern branch shown on the map from Maryville to Chilhowee was extended to Calderwood the following year (1915).

21

A lesson in ice cream

Everett Whaley of Sevier County says he saw and ate his first ice cream at the Elkmont commissary in 1915. He was seven years old.

Everett's family lived then at the head of Sugarland Branch, across Sugarland Mountain and five miles from Elkmont. The ice cream came from Knoxville by train.

Everett had several nickels he'd saved and decided he'd buy a cone each for two younger brothers, Frank and Arnold, who had stayed home.

He says he didn't realize ice cream would melt. It was a hot summer day and as he walked along he soon learned how temporary ice cream could be.

His older brother Harold, who knew something about ice cream, yelled back to him grinning, "You might as well eat it. You'll never carry it home."

Everett bought ice cream for his brothers and not for his sisters because the sisters weren't yet born. Leander C. and Ruth Conner Whaley had five sons in a row, Harold, Everett, Frank, Arnold, and Eugene, followed by three daughters, Helen, Nan, and Charlotte.

Photo by Vic Weals
Burea and Everett Whaley, in 1985 photo, walk a section of the trail that he walked to his first ice cream cone 70 years earlier. The scene is near the Sugarlands Visitor Center of the Great Smoky Mountains National Park, above Gatlinburg.

Lavern Massey on the porch of the home she and Fred built years after they returned to Wears Valley. The back yard is at the border of Great Smoky Mountains National Park, Cove Mountain rising steeply behind.

22

Farewell forever to Hood Siding

Lavern Massey was paid $100 a week by Little River Lumber Co. to feed the 18 workers she cooked for in the camp at Hood Siding.

She paid the kitchen help and bought the food out of the $100. Still she cleared about half of it in profit most weeks, and fed the men well enough that they didn't complain.

Lavern's husband Jack at the same time was earning his separate salary as engineer on a log train. Together they netted $75 to $100 each week. And $75 in 1921 was maybe more than what several hundred dollars a week would be later in her life. "We made real good money for that day," she said.

From left, Forest Ogle, Jack Massey, and Pink Ownby were the crew of a Shay locomotive on East Prong in the 1920s.

Jack helped with the work, before and after train runs. For instance he milked the cow twice a day that provided most of the milk, butter and coffee cream. During a stretch when their own cow was dry they bought milk from the nearby Bill Abbott family.

Their dog Mollie and a pet groundhog are between Jack and Lavern Massey at their company-owned house at Elkmont.

They also had their store of home-canned vegetables. But provisions were so cheap that they could have bought everything and fed the men well and still shown a profit.

Bacon was 10 cents a pound; white flour for bread and biscuits, 50 cents for 50 pounds; cornmeal, 50 cents a bushel. They raised and canned green beans, grew and stored a potato crop.

For breakfast she fixed coffee, bacon and eggs, gravy, and oversize biscuits formed from dough with the end of an empty peach can. "I had a biscuit pan that held 24, and I'd bake it twice full every morning," Lavern said.

"I didn't make any pan pies—I made cobbler pies all the time, in a dutch oven. I couldn't have baked enough pan pies to feed that whole bunch. Some would have eaten nothing but pie. Most of the cobblers were apple, but I also made berry and peach."

Did anybody ever get seconds?

"Oh yes, if there was any pie left over, and there was most of the time, they were welcome to it if they wanted it."

Breakfast and supper in the winter months were eaten by the light of oil lamps spaced around the kitchen-dining car. Meal preparation and dishwashing were done by the same light, for there was no electrical service at Hood Siding.

Water to do the dishes would be heating on the stove while they ate. Most evenings there'd be enough volunteers to wash and dry the dishes and put them away.

After supper almost everybody gathered in the other railroad car. It too had a stove, a coal burner. They'd sit on the wooden benches around it and in their talk they would live again their day in the logging woods.

Finally somebody would remind that it was bedtime, and the boarders would say goodnight to the Massey family and go to their own lonely little bunkhouses scattered nearby.

Hood Siding was a busy, noisy place in the daytime in the years Lavern and Jack worked there. At least two mixed trains a day passed on runs between Walland and Elkmont. And there were log trains passing, or stopping to load the big timber that was being harvested on Meigs Creek and winched down across the river on the swinging railroad bridge.

Jack and Lavern and their infant son stayed in the lobby car, in bedrooms partitioned at one end. They lived there until after their son's first birthday.

With the river and the main line of the railroad right at hand, there was no safe outdoor place for the child to play. Their doctor advised them to get away from there.

"I doubt I'll stay here after you leave," one of the men told Lavern after she broke the news. "We won't ever again have a mess that's fit to eat," he told her.

Lavern recalled that she did leave with regret. She enjoyed cooking for men who appreciated her effort. And she liked the profit of it.

The Masseys moved around the mountain into Wears Valley, into an ancient log house on the farm owned by Lavern's parents, Houston and Texana Lawson.

There in the hollow under the north slope of Cove Mountain they started what for Jack was a new career—farming. He completely quit his job with Little River and never went back to it, and in fact never wanted to do anything but farm after that, Lavern said.

Never did they leave Wears Valley again. The other four of their five children were born there, and Jack died there in 1974, soon after they'd moved into a new home.

Vic Olson operated a log crane on Little River, and sometimes shared laughs with Jess Cole. The picture is of Olson and an unidentified companion.

23

Work with Jess, laugh with Jess

Lumberjacks are often thought of as heroic figures, of legendary size and strength. There were at least some in that mold who worked for the Little River Lumber Co. in the Great Smoky Mountains.

The brothers Len and Ave Cogdill are remembered as being about six feet, six inches tall, and of powerful build along with it. Then, at a height of 66 inches, or 12 inches shorter than the Cogdills, there was Jess Cole. Mutt and Jeff, they called Len and Jess, who worked on the same skidder crew for a time.

Most of the men on the Little River job ranged somewhere between in size. Many started so young they hadn't reached their full growth, weren't yet shaving regularly. The job, though, was man-size, and what they all had in common, from tallest to smallest, was that they could handle it. Jess, when he was past 80 and living on Waldens Creek Road out of Pigeon Forge, answered a few questions about himself, and his memories of life in the logging camps above Elkmont.

Do you have a middle name, Jess?

"No. There's so many of us in the family they just barely had a name apiece for us."

You've been married to your wife, Beedie Carr, for how many years?

"For 54 years to the same woman. If a man tries to outlive just one, he's up against a proposition."

What are some of the jobs you've worked at, Jess?

Jess Cole in lumberjack days

"Well, I was a foreman for the Little River Lumber Co. nine years on a straight, 11 years altogether. I cooked some at Gatlinburg hotels and in the logging camps. I did carpenter work and laid stone the last 10 years."

You must have been one of the smaller foremen working for Little River.

"Yes, they called me Shorty. But I raised more foremen for the Little River Lumber people than anybody else ever did. I'd take a man on and work him until he learned to skid and learned to rig and everything, and then recommend him for foreman."

People say you got along well with the men who worked under you.

"I kept a crowd of boys, all the time, nearly, and if you'd come up on the job you couldn't tell who was foreman. We all worked just alike, scuffled and cut up and acted the fool.

"I worked just as hard as any man I had, and I wouldn't let a green man get in a close place—dangerous place, you know. Rigging trees and stuff like that I'd do myself. We rigged a big spruce up there one time—it was about 75 feet high and on top of a cliff. If a man fell out of it he'd fall 150 feet, I guess.

"Them boys sitting on the ground and telling me what to do and how to do. And I said I'm foreman and have to do all the work and these green hands tell me what to do.

"The main skidder super came up there and said if you'll top that tree I'll give you half a day for it. It was on Saturday and we liked to come out home early Saturday evening if we could get to. It was dinner time then. He was going in to dinner when he told me that. (Dinner in the country in those days was the noon meal.) "I said if I can get this landing man's axe I'll top that tree and be in before you finish eating. And I sure enough did but I sure enough got scared. It was so straight up you didn't know which way it was going to fall, up the hill or down, the top of it.

"So I first took a rope and tied myself up there. Then I think to myself why, if that tree was to split open, that rope'd cut me in two. And I took the rope off and stood on two limbs.

"Of course you know how a spruce is. The limbs is thick on it. I chopped it and it just commenced r-r-rocking and directly it went off below the fill, and I did get off before they got through eating dinner.

"Back then, to get half a day off was something. Because we worked six days a week, and for about three years we worked 11 hours to the day and got paid for 10. We commenced at six, took an hour for dinner and quit at six. I told them I was living on the job and never got to see my wife in daylight. I told them I was going to swap my bed for a lantern, because I had to go out before day and come in after dark."

Jess, do you believe a small man makes as good a foreman on a logging operation as a big man does?

"Ordinarily a small man is stronger to his size than a big man is. I used to weigh about 138 or 139, along there, winter and summer. I'd offer to wrestle or box with anybody in camp within 20 pounds of my weight. Of course where there's 75 or 80 men in the camp you'll get a call once in a while.

"The hardest scuffling I ever had was with a boy that weighed in the same notch I did. We used to have a saying, you know, that if you weighed in the same notch you had to wrestle. We commenced I guess about 15 minutes before work time. Ten minutes after work time we was still wrestling. Nary one of us could put the other's back down. The coal pile was right there and we got in it. We finally wound up in a little old creek branch."

Who was that you scuffled with?

"Elmer Reagan. Me and him stayed on the same skidder most of the time. They called me the little buck and him the little engineer. He was all man. He was stout as a bear to his size."

You said something about, if you weighed in the same notch. You mean on those old platform scales?

"Yes. We weighed 138 pounds apiece. I had weighed and then he came in on the job and said he weighed 138 pound. I said, well, me and you got to wrestle. We could put it off till morning.

"Next morning we went to work a little early and we tangled up, both laughing all the time. I was a little quicker than he was. I could make it hard on him, but couldn't put his shoulders down and hold him there."

Were there many practical jokes played around a logging camp?

"I was hooking tongs one day when the superintendent, Ed Ijams, brought a bunch of women up there to look over the job. We was loading off a trestle and Vic Olson, the Swede who ran the loader, saw the women coming but let on like he didn't. When they got up right even with a big mudhole there, Vic dropped that big log in it. Boy, they looked like they'd been drug through the mud.

"He wheeled his loader around and said, 'Hel-lo, Mr. Ijams, I didn't see you.' Then he turned his loader around the other way and was just dying laughing."

The Cole front porch was often crowded on Sunday afternoons with old logging camp friends who came to enjoy him once more. Jess died a short time after this interview of May 1976.

Splash at center of picture was logs hitting the water of the storage pond as the train at left was being unloaded. Fire destroyed the Townsend sawmill (out of the picture and to the right) three times through the years, and a common joke was that it burned everything but the log pond.

24

Sam and Alva Henry

The lumber company's most remote commissary for a time was about five miles above Elkmont, where Fish Camp Prong flows into Little River. Sam Henry moved there to manage the store in 1912, and wife Alva went with him. All three of their children were born there or at Elkmont in the next four years—two sons and a daughter.

Sam owned a Kodak roll film camera and kept it busy. The black bear was plentiful around Three Forks in the first years, and Sam tried to photograph them all. He was most excited at a chance to snap a mother bear and cubs.

From Three Forks the Henrys moved downriver to Elkmont, where he became postmaster and company paymaster after 1914. On weekends he also wore the hat of woods boss while the full-time bosses sojourned elsewhere. When weekend drinking and fighting made the camps above Elkmont dangerous places to be, it was Sam who organized baseball teams among the loggers, to play teams from Sevierville, Gatlinburg, and Townsend, along with other places within reasonable commuting distance. Sam's effort didn't eliminate the drinking and violence, but it eased it some.

Reminiscing about his parents in 1989, Paul Henry said their picture collection was one of the pleasures of their later years, to Sam's death in 1971 and Alva's in 1979.

Vic Weals photo, 1962

Sam and Alva Henry enjoyed the pictures they collected in more than 50 years of living on Little River, first at Three Forks and Elkmont, and the final years at Townsend.

Alva allowed the collection to be copied more than once after Sam's death, and some have appeared in area historical publications. The Henrys often bought pictures from itinerant photographers, many with good detail of locomotives, log trains, skidder sets, mountainsides stripped of timber, wrecked equipment and working equipment. There are prints of Jim Shelton pictures but few photographs of Sam Henry, himself.

Henry collection photos

Running the company store at Three Forks was Sam Henry's first job with the lumber company. Railroad to right was a long one up Fish Camp Prong. Track at left continued up Little River in the direction of Clingmans Dome.

The Henry family moved from Elkmont to Townsend in 1923, where Sam was postmaster and bookkeeper of Townsend Mercantile Co. until he retired in 1952. I enjoyed several letters from Sam through the years, and don't remember a misspelled word or an awkward sentence in any of them.

Samuel W. Henry's letters and photographs have become an important chronicle of life on Little River in the 20th Century.

Frame building housed the commissary, Elkmont post office, and a small transient hotel. Sam Henry is at right.

25

A place to live

Timber was cut and camps set up in some remote places before the railroad arrived. A log bunkhouse and kitchen above Elkmont were built and furnished with what could be hand-carried up the mountain. Luther Dockery lived and worked at this one, and the picture is from his son, Gaston. Luther died when the son was a small boy.

26

The new bookkeeper from Trade

Little River Lumber Co. in its less than 40 years of existence cut more than 750 million board feet of timber.

It wore out 10 locomotives, three log loaders, several incline machines, two steam shovels, one ditcher, five steam-powered overhead skidders, and about 75 railroad flatcars.

It employed more than 600 men at one time at the peak of its operation. The total number who came and went, from the company's start in 1901 until final shutdown in 1940, totals well into the thousands.

Stuart P. McNiell, superintendent of Little River in its final years and a Blount County resident for the rest of his life, gathered these facts from company records and from people who were there when it happened.

Stuart P. McNiell beside the last trainload of logs delivered from Middle Prong to the mill at Townsend, in 1938.

McNiell came to Townsend and the Little River Lumber Co. in 1922 as a bookkeeper. He was 23 years old and the company had already been operating 21 years. It was at its peak of production, or close to it.

He was born in Tennessee's easternmost village, Trade, in Johnson County against the North Carolina line. His father, Walter A. McNiell, was a medical doctor there.

Young Stuart was drafted for World War I on the day it ended, Nov. 11,

1918. Soon he was out of uniform again and teaching school in Johnson County. His graduation from Draughon's Business College in Knoxville earned him a teaching job at Draughon's in Memphis. Soon he traveled back to upper East Tennessee to Hampton in Carter County, where he worked in the office for Pittsburgh Lumber Co.

From Hampton he was invited by the late Dock Tipton, then superintendent of Little River, to come to work at Townsend. That he did in September of 1922. In 1925 McNiell married Stella Myers, a descendant of Tuckaleechee Cove's pioneer families.

In the several years before his death in 1984, Mac gathered pictures and a considerable history of the railroad and lumber company, and shared them generously with many others in the same quest.

Young Stella Myers and the lumber company's new Reo rail car. She later married S.P. McNiell.

27

These boots were made for logging

C alked boots could be a deadly weapon when the men who wore them fought, if one got the other down and stomped him.

The calks were also pronounced "corks," but by any name they were dozens of sharp steel points embedded in the sole and heel of each boot. In the words of Elbert Wilkey they were as "sure-footed as a squirrel's claw" for leaping from log to log.

Elbert Wilkey, surveyor and forester, had his calked boots rebuilt after wearing them 17 years.

Most loggers thought they had to have a pair, and until World War I the cost was about a week's wages, a week's work being 10 or 11 hours a day for six days. As late as 1928, one of the more prosperous years of the Roaring Twenties, outfitters in the Southern mountains sold them at $16 to $18 a pair, still a big chunk of a week's pay.

They were called "cutter boots," or cutters, as often as they were called calked boots, and many men thought of them as an investment. Owning a pair made it easier to be hired for work around log landings, and boots in good condition could be sold or pawned readily for cash in emergencies.

"Three-Day Jimmy" earned the nickname by working only briefly at each place that hired him, and soon ran out of commissaries that would sell him boots on credit. Jimmy was good at building railroad trestles of hemlock logs, and it was to walk the peeled logs that he needed the cutter boots.

The Wilkey brothers began life in the mountain logging camps where their father, a skidder operator, was employed. Elbert, Howard, and James, oldest to youngest, are pictured about a mile above the mouth of Slickrock in 1917.

Herbert Trentham's first calked cutter boots were home-made with the help of horseshoe nails. Trentham was a stout boy nine years old when he first pulled one end of a two-man crosscut saw, cutting timber for Andy Huff near Gatlinburg. It was sometime later that he and his co-workers cut the heads from horseshoe nails, and drove them into the heels of their boots to make them nonskid.

Trentham says that when a beef was killed in that Smoky Mountain neighborhood, it was a practice to save the fat and render it to tallow. "We'd lay our boots by the fire until they got real hot. Then we'd rub them good with a chunk of that tallow. Now you talk about something that would turn snow water, they would," Trentham says.

Elbert Wilkey owned several pairs of store-bought cutters while he was an employee of the U.S. Forest Service. He says they were the best possible footwear to keep him from slipping and falling while carrying expensive and fragile survey instruments.

118

He paid $65 for a favorite pair late in the 1960s, and wore them 17 years before they needed rebuilding. The White Shoe Co. of Spokane, Wash., did the job for $155, installing new soles and heels with new calks implanted. Only the tough uppers, still impervious to rattlesnake bite and sawbriars, remain of the original boots.

Since retirement from the Forest Service Wilkey has lived at Enka, N.C., where he continues a private practice as a land surveyor. Trentham lives at Gatlinburg, Tenn., retired from his main life's work as a Smokies tour guide and driver.

– Photo from Sam Henry

The Clyde skidder was one of five owned by Little River Lumber Co. In the scene pictured it was ready to move to a new location, after doing its job of hauling logs from the slopes to the railroad. A loading crew would move in next, the men wearing calked boots for surer footing as they leaped from log to log.

Loading . . .

Loaded!

The two larger pictures on the page at left were kept for many years by Robert Houser, who used them to explain to his family the kind of work he once did for the Little River Lumber Co.

Robert lived more than 90 years, and spent most of the last of it farming at his place on Mill Creek out of Pigeon Forge. He died in 1978.

The photographs are from his wife Nora and sons Marion Houser of Mill Creek, Muncy of Gatlinburg and Manford of Maryville.

The steam-powered log crane ran on rails on top of the flatcars. The rails stayed there. The short section of transfer rails to get the loader from one car to the next stayed with the loader.

A single, slender steel cable lifted the log. Sometimes a cable snapped under its load, and when it did it might slice everything in its path.

The logs in the pictures look to have been 16 feet long, a standard length. They appear to have weighed in the range of 1,600 to 1,800 pounds each. Timber recently cut weighed heaviest.

When the tongs were hooked into a log, they had to be placed about midway of its length, at the center of balance, so the log would ride level as it was being lifted to the flatcar.

Three big logs were put in the bottom row, and two big ones were loaded into the second row. The chains were then tightened over those five logs, and secured to hooks on the side of the car.

Then a heavy log, unchained, was loaded onto the top of the pile. Its weight helped keep the chains beneath it taut.

The operator of the log loader needed skill to guide a free-swinging log into place on the car. Sometimes he bumped the log against the car to angle it in the desired direction.

The top loader was the man who freed the tongs from the log after it was lowered into its place. He did this by hitting the tongs from above with his peavey. It took a forceful, well-placed lick to loosen them from the log.

The tong hooker was the worker on the log landing who caught the tongs as they were swung toward him at the end of the cable. The loaderman would swing the machine and play out cable at the same time, and he could "throw" the tongs 35 to 40 feet or more.

Tong hookers and top loaders both wore boots with calks. A tong hooker traveled through the jumble of logs at the landing by leaping from one log to the next. He could jump eight feet or more and land sure-footed on a log that was peeled and slippery. Sometimes a log would be so heavy that it would overbalance the steam log loader and topple it from the flatcar. So the job of the operator was also dangerous.

The flatcar closest to the locomotive was loaded first. Usually there were four flatcars in one log train, but sometimes there were as many as eight on the gentler forest grades.

There were two piles or "bunks" of logs on each car. That meant about 12 logs to the car when the trees were of a size pictured here.

George Perryman (at left) and an unidentified companion wore calked boots in their work at a log landing.

When the last car was loaded, the operator backed the log loader onto its own flatcar to wait for the next train of empties.

If it was a long wait he might have mechanical maintenance to do, or lunch to eat.

If there was a stream nearby, and there usually was, he might do some trout fishing.

Or maybe he'd shoot squirrels, if there were any trees left standing in the neighborhood.

28

Stringtown mourns Pete McCarter

Pete McCarter was 15 years old when he was killed at work on Middle Prong of Little River in 1926. Pete was a "flagman" who relayed signals for the men who worked on No. 4 skidder.

Although it was a job with responsibilities, it was considered a beginner's for payroll purposes, and Pete had hope of moving up to something better.

No. 4 skidder fell over one day and was having to be jacked back into position. Big jacks of the kind used to put railroad cars back on the tracks were to be used, and Pete volunteered to work one of the jacks. He may have seen it as a step toward a better job. When one opened up, it would be his if the bosses thought he could do it.

– Photo from Marjorie Ownby
Pete McCarter shortly before his death at the age of 15 on Middle Prong.

"It was what we called a latch jack," Pete's younger brother Raleigh McCarter recalled. Raleigh was 11 years old in 1926 and remembered Pete's death very clearly.

"He forgot to set the latch on the jack. When he turned the handle loose it flew up and hit him under the chin, It broke his neck. He never did know what happened to him," Raleigh said.

Raymer Brackin came walking by a short time after Pete died. It was close to the end of the work day, and all the skidder crew and most of the residents of the nearby camp were gathered there. Pete's father, H. Newt McCarter, had been summoned and was sitting, weeping, head in hand beside his dead son, Raymer said. Raleigh said their mother, Esther Moore McCarter, never did completely recover from the sadness of the day.

It happened at the mouth of 'Coon Branch near a little logging camp called Stringtown. There were many stringtowns in the mountains through

String of portable houses at Three Forks, above Elkmont.

the years. Wherever the little portable shanties were lined up beside the railroad, it might be called Stringtown.

Wilma Cope Williamson, daughter of Fred and Dora Cope, was there the day Pete died. "It happened almost in our front yard," she recalled. Wilma had gone to school with Pete, and although he was somewhat older she knew him well. She remembered him as a shy person, "not rowdy like some boys at his age."

Pete's death affected the whole camp. "I had nightmares over it for days after that," Wilma said. Her sister Edith Cope Fox remembered Pete being dressed for burial in a starched white shirt and a pair of bib overalls. His grave is in the Walker Cemetery in Walker Valley, near the Tremont Environmental Center and down the valley from where he was killed. Pete was a nickname, and his grave stone bears the name his parents gave him, W. Wesley McCarter.

The picture of Pete came from a cousin, Marjorie Ownby. His brother Raleigh said there were five sons and a daughter in the family and that three of them survived in 1983: Ray in Texas; Harvey in Florida; and Raleigh, retired and living in Maryville. Hobart Proffitt was crushed when a log rolled from an incline car, in that same neighborhood and three months after Pete was killed. Proffitt was 31 years old and left a wife and children. Grace Etherton, a relative, said he was taken home to the Glades east of Gatlinburg to be buried in the Proffitt Cemetery.

The function of a skidder was to haul logs from the slopes via overhead cable. One could strip a mountainside in a few days.

The trees with deep-fissured bark in foreground were chestnut, photographed in 1910 on Little Santeetlah Creek south of the Smokies. The chestnuts are gone, from blight or old age, and the site is now Joyce Kilmer Memorial Forest.

29

Death of the American chestnut forest and new hope for its resurrection

W ill Effler hunted mostly on West Fork of Little River, on the north slope of Thunderhead Mountain late in the 19th Century and early in the 20th. Will used a muzzleload rifle to the end of his life.

His daughter Anna Effler Maples recalled that Will owned four such rifles, kept hanging on pegs where the younger of 11 Effler children couldn't reach them, in the loft of their home in Dry Valley near the border of what is now Great Smoky Mountains National Park.

Will Effler and Margaret Sullivan Effler. After a life as a Smoky Mountain hunter and guide, Will died at 50. After 11 children, Margaret lived past 70.

If Effler was hunting bear he'd pour the barrel "about half-full of gunpowder," Anna said, so he could kill the animal with one shot. If he was hunting turkey or smaller game he'd pour a small amount of powder.

Effler told of watching two big flocks of wild turkeys feast on fallen chestnuts on Defeat Ridge one autumn afternoon. He trailed the flocks to their separate roosting places at dusk.

He shot one big bird that evening, dressed it, and counted 92 chestnuts, still in the hulls and undigested, out of its craw. Early next morning he went to the other roost and killed another gobbler of about equal size. But when he dressed it he found no chestnuts in that bird's craw. They had been ground up and digested while the turkey roosted, during the night. A few hours earlier there would have been maybe about the same number of chestnuts as in the first bird.

This all happened when the native American chestnut tree made up more than 25 percent of the Smoky Mountain forest, before the lumber companies came, and before a fungus blight killed what were left and kept the young growth from ever maturing again.

There were trees so big that one of them would drop 10 or more bushels of chestnuts, and in the words of John McCaulley, the Cades Cove turkey hunter, "the earth would be black with chestnuts." A turkey on any given day would eat all it could hold, and the fat it built up on the autumn bonanza would help it survive the hungrier winter days ahead.

Herbert M. Webster was at left at end of the file of chestnut hunters who climbed to Thunderhead Mountain in October 1928. The Knoxville group left home poorly prepared in that there were only two or three cloth sacks and one lard can in the crowd. They filled all pockets, made sacks of shirts and undershirts, filled every container they could contrive. The scene was a chestnut grove at the fringe of Thunderhead, and the trunks littering it were of trees killed by the blight.

Earl Cady called the chestnut crop a banquet table for wildlife. Along with the turkey, all the squirrel species and the woods rat, the white-footed woodland mouse, the bear, deer and raccoon gorged themselves on chestnuts in the fall and stored layers of fat in their bodies to sustain them through the winter. The feast enabled the mammalian females to nourish larger and healthier litters of young, Cady said. The chestnut crop each fall was so dependable it almost never failed as a food source for wildlife. Chestnuts were the seed of the tree, so abundant that the future of the chestnut forest appeared to be guaranteed. But although it might have recovered in the wake of the cut-and-run logger, the American chestnut species was soon dead or dying from a fungus imported accidentally from Asia.

The disease was first detected in this country in 1904 on trees in New York Zoological Park, probably infected from nursery seedlings brought from Japan. It spread so rapidly in the New York area that five years later it had destroyed 16,000 trees at the edge of Brooklyn—every native American chestnut tree in Forest Park. A news story in the New York Times of May 14, 1909, lamented the loss:

– **Emert family photo**

Ira and Belle Emert, at right, from Walland, and other family members camped among the big chestnut trees at the shoulder of Spence Field in the 1920s. Trees struck by lightning, or dying from the great chestnut blight then sweeping America, provided abundant wood for their campfire.

"The once dense forests of Forest Park now present a sad sight to lovers of nature. Everywhere once beautiful and stately chestnuts stand gaunt and lifeless against the green of other trees, like ghosts of the forest. Many have been felled by the woodmen, but thousands still stand, naked and gray and dead, where oaks and maples and birches display the green glory which spring has brought to them.

"'We discovered that the scourge was attacking the trees in the park five years ago (in 1904),' Park Commissioner Michael J. Kennedy said yesterday. 'We did everything possible to arrest the spread of the disease, but there seems to be no cure. It attacks the trees inside the bark, and there apparently is no way of treating them.'"

As is often true with imported pests and blights, the chestnut fungus became much more virulent in America than it had been in its native land, where a natural resistance in China, Korea, and Japan allowed the Asian chestnut to live and continue bearing.

Wind, birds, and insects and possibly other carriers spread the blight quickly across America over great distances. If a valley was bypassed and spared from infection temporarily, the fungus almost inevitably came back to it from another direction.

Estimates by the U.S. Department of Agriculture were that all the chestnut trees in their natural range across the Eastern United States would equal nine million acres of nothing but chestnut. A related estimate early in the 20th Century was that chestnut trees were 28 percent of the timber on 33 million acres in the Southern Appalachians. Some Smoky Mountain valleys were as much as 40 percent chestnut.

The blight hadn't yet struck the Smokies when the Little River Lumber Co. began to log the pristine forest of West Prong, where chestnut timber was

Stinnett family photo
Kate Duggan, at left, from Eusebia, taught at Walker Valley School in an age when the students brought chestnuts to eat as a snack at recess. From left, the Walker Valley family pictured with Kate were Alex, Martha, and Elizabeth Stinnett; their mother, Mary Stinnett; another son, Howard Taft Stinnett.

so plentiful that the large areas of Lower Chestnut Flats and Upper Chestnut Flats were named for it. So much chestnut was hauled to Townsend in the lumber company's first years that nothing but chestnut would be scheduled to the band saws for days without letup.

Howard Stinnett said it was 1925, the year of a long dry spell and record hot weather in East Tennessee, that the chestnut blight became suddenly serious in Walker Valley. "The leaves turned brown before fall that year, on the trees along the ridges, and at first we thought it was the drought. It hadn't rained in weeks. But it turned out to be the blight, and that was the end of the chestnut trees. They died fast after 1925," Howard said.

A tree at the upper end of Townsend, on the William A. Myers place, showered its bounty on throngs of people through the years, until the blight killed it. "That was about the most famous tree around Townsend when I was a boy. People felt free to go there and pick up chestnuts, and it was the biggest chestnut tree I've ever seen. The trunk was about eight feet through," Howard said.

East of Defeat Ridge in the timber-rich valley of Sams Creek off Thunderhead Prong in the 1930s, Raymer Brackin helped cut dead or dying chestnut trees that were "four or five feet through." They were good for lumber, and all sent to the mill to be sawed if they weren't hollow.

Lillard McCarter remembered days when every log would be chestnut, in the trails of logs he snaked down the hollows of Lynn Camp Prong and Thunderhead Prong, driving horse teams for John Ownby.

American chestnut wood resisted rot and stood up under the weather, a reason that long slender chestnut poles were bought in quantity by the telephone and electric companies. American Telephone & Telegraph Co. began to stockpile the poles when it became apparent that there soon would be no more new-growth chestnut. Big construction timbers sawed from chestnut were in demand also because they stood the weather, and because they were lighter in weight than oak timbers.

Harbor pilings, mine props, fence posts, and railroad ties were of chestnut because it was abundant, relatively cheap, and resistant to rot. The furniture industry was a customer for chestnut because the lumber was light in weight, easily sawed and worked, and attractive when finished and varnished. It was a favorite wood for the manufacture of coffins, before metal caskets became common. Straight-grained American chestnut was easily split into rails, the material of farm fences from pioneer times on. Sills and other timbers laid close to the ground in mountain homes and barns were often of chestnut.

Earl R. Cady came from the University of Michigan's forestry graduate school to the Smokies in 1937, as an assistant to Arthur Stupka in the first year of the new national park's ranger-naturalist programs. Thousands of dead chestnut trees still standing in 1937 were a reminder that the blight was the greatest local forest disaster ever. Cady later served with Tennessee Valley Authority, Kentucky Game and Fish Commission, as an extension forester and teacher at the University of Tennessee, and as a forest management consultant.

In 1990, living in Maryville and semiretired from professional pursuits,

Cady continued his lifetime habits of hiking and fishing the mountain trout streams, and looking along the way for chestnut growth that might show promise of being blight-resistant. What he found through the years was the false hope of small green sprouts from chestnut root systems that had been dead above ground for more than a half-century. Seldom did he find sprouts as large as one or two inches in diameter.

"As long as the stem bark is smooth, these young sprouts and saplings are immune to the blight," Cady observed. "But when perpendicular striations (cracks) begin to appear in the maturing bark, the blight fungi invade the stems and the above-ground part of the plant dies."

Cady and other chestnut watchers meanwhile have been given new hope that the sprouts could still help restore the chestnut tree to the Smoky Mountain forests, perhaps to be the area's dominant

– Photo by Vic Weals

Earl R. Cady fishing below Bald River Falls, on Cherokee National Forest southwest of the Smokies.

hardwood species again, although that would come well into the 21st Century or later, with many ifs and maybes along the road. Keith Langdon, natural resources specialist at Great Smoky Mountains National Park headquarters near Gatlinburg, talked about the park's role in chestnut research in 1990.

"American chestnut was our most common tree at mid-elevations of the park. There are still a lot of stumps around, but most of the stumps from the older trees haven't resprouted. We think that the majority of the sprouts we have are from what could be called 'old seedlings,' trees that were small when they were hit by the blight.

"Sprouts are still common, and where the sunlight reaches these remnant root sprouts, like along power lines and roadways, they sometimes get large enough to flower. What we're doing is collecting twigs from the sprouts, twigs about the diameter of a pencil or smaller, in a cooperative arrangement with the University of Tennessee Department of Forestry, Wildlife and Fisheries. We've provided a number of twigs from known individual chestnuts in the park, to be grafted to American chestnut root stock from other sites. We don't know where the root stock is from, but it provides a good grafting base for the Smokies chestnut stock.

"The objective of all this is a subset of what's going on nationally, where they've found that most of the breeding work done by the government early in the century was perhaps done incorrectly, and it failed to produce a blight-resistant American chestnut. By using modern breeding techniques we can make an initial cross with the Oriental chestnut, which is highly resistant. Then we can take the hybrid and inoculate it with the blight after it reaches several years old, and kill off the offspring that don't have the resistant genes. At this point we have resistant trees that are half Oriental and half American.

"We hope to breed these back to American chestnuts for three successive generations, inoculating them at each stage after they're several years old. Eventually what we wind up with is a resistant generation that is around 95 percent American stock. Most of the trees through the different steps will die, but at the end we'll have trees that are 95 percent American chestnut from the Smokies.

"What we're looking for besides blight resistance is desirable timber characteristics and shade tolerance and aggressive growth like the American chestnut had. It's a project that will take years, maybe 20 years or more, and we're not absolutely sure it's going to work."

If a blight-resistant tree is developed that is mostly American chestnut, will the National Park Service plant it in the Smokies to try to return it to the dominance it had here early in the 20th Century?

Not automatically, Langdon said. "First off, in our national park policy we have a prohibition to establishing things in the park that are alien or exotic. We've had so many problems with exotic plants and animals, it's the No. 1 problem in the national park system as a whole. So we haven't guaranteed that we're going to reestablish the chestnut, even if the hybrid research works. We're just going to evaluate it at the end of this long-term project.

"We do not believe that we would have to clear areas to plant it. The evidence we have seen in Wisconsin is that this tree is capable on its own of reinvading total shade, and dominating the site in just a few years. The American chestnut can make it on its own, if it can be freed from the blight.

"That's where the park is trying to help, but we had a major setback last December (1989) when the early freeze hit the grafts before they had hardened off at the University of Tennessee facility. So we're having to collect almost all of our wood over again. We have the trees located and tagged out in the forest, and that makes it a lot easier to start over again.

"This coming March (1991) we'll be gathering that material. We're doing it in collaboration with Dr. Scott Schlarbaum at the University of Tennessee. The American Chestnut Foundation is spearheading the effort nationally, and Phil Rutter is president of that. The foundation has established an experimental farm near Abingdon, Va.

"The other strategy that is being pursued is one that has worked very well in Europe, where their chestnut was decimated by the same disease.

Their chestnut has since come back because races of the same fungus with lower virulence have overcome the more virulent kind. The trees still get cankered, but they heal over, and they're able to produce nuts."

Of other forest growth that has come back in the more than half-century since the lumber company departed, Langdon said:

"It will be a long time before the vegetation structure is recreated—the complex layers of growth that were there before the loggers cut it. Stumps of some species have sprouted rather well, and other species have reseeded.

"In very old growth forest here in the park, researchers have discovered that there is a little bit more than one percent of loss of the forest canopy each year. This creates a natural patchwork of openings in the old growth, where big trees have come down, that is good for wildlife.

"The big change we have seen is in the unprecedented number of forest diseases that have appeared. The chestnut blight was only the first. We're losing the fir, of course, to an introduced insect. A fungus has stopped the butternuts from reproducing, and probably the ones we have now are the only ones we'll see. They've been made a federal candidate for endangered species protection.

"There are other problems. You've probably noticed the elms along Little River, where hundreds of them have died in the second wave of Dutch elm disease. There's an insect headed this way called the hemlock wooly adelgid, which seems to be doing a good job of infecting the hemlocks in Shenandoah National Park. We have a large number of problems that have been introduced to this country from sister species of trees in the Orient or in Europe. We're not sure how these diseases are going to affect forest succession on Little River or in other cut-over areas."

Langdon said the yellow poplar, or tuliptree, has come back especially strong in old cultivated fields, as in the Sugarlands above Gatlinburg, where impressive stands of their straight and towering trunks can be seen from the highway. There are poplars throughout the lower elevation forests of the park, and they dominate some of the areas that were open and sunlit, either as cornfields or cut-over timberlands, a half-century earlier.

"We are counting on the yellow poplars to help keep the gypsy moth in check locally in some of these areas," Langdon said. "The gypsy moth will be here in a few years, and the poplar is not something the gypsy moth will eat. They don't eat poplars or ash, and they don't bother a few other species."

Photo by Vic Weals, 1951

The tall, slender trees were young yellow poplars reaching for the sun in 1951, trying to reclaim the site where Little Greenbrier School was built of poplar logs 70 years earlier. Former students came to a "working" to clear the underbrush in 1952, so that reunions could be held on the grounds.

Photo by Vic Weals, 1952

Only five yellow poplar logs were needed for each wall of the Little Greenbrier School. The timbers were shaped with axes, except that the ends and corner notches were sawed. The Rev. C.C. Oliver held an ax for size comparison. The building near the Sevier-Blount County line still stood in 1991, maintained by the National Park Service as a relic of the past.

Photo by Vic Weals, 1962

Louisa Walker breaking beans on the front porch was the last of the six spinster Walker sisters who lived out their lives in the cabin built by their grandparents in Little Greenbrier Cove. The house was of yellow poplar logs that were relatively small in size, possibly because there was not enough manpower at hand to lift bigger timbers.

The farm fence in foreground, of split chestnut rails and poles, was one inherited by the Park Service when it acquired most of Cades Cove in the 1930s, although many families were by then fencing with wire. The ranger was Charles S. Dunn, Dry Valley native who was one of the first assigned to the Smokies. Dunn later became founding superintendent of Chickamauga and Chattanooga National Military Park.

Photo from C.S. Dunn

Oak and a few chestnut trees still stood in 1934 in a stand that had been mostly chestnut, until the blight greatly thinned the forest at the shoulder of Spence Field. Picture documented the abundance of grass in the last year the Park Service allowed livestock grazing here.

McCauley family photo

The herder's cabin between Gregory Bald and Parson Bald was in a grove of chestnut trees, some of them showing in background. Whole families gathered chestnuts here in the fall, and John McCauley told of seeing 100 bushel piled up at the cabin, with four men busy daily hauling them off the mountain on pack mules. They were hauled from the lower Cove to Knoxville in wagons, to be sold to buyers there. Many went to street vendors in Eastern cities, to be roasted and sold from pushcarts.

Photo from Jasper Morrow

A chestnut tree brought down by the blight made a grandstand seat for G.W. Morrow in Moss Gap, as he viewed the panorama of the Unicoi Mountains south of the Smokies in 1918. Pointed peak in center distance is Waucheesi Mountain in Monroe County, Tenn.

141

Branches of dead chestnut at left frame the view of another dying chestnut at the fringe of Russell Field, west of Thunderhead Mountain on the main ridge of the Smokies in 1915. The mountaintop was one of the treeless meadows of the Smokies, where livestock grazing and limited farming were conducted.

Homemade chestnut coffin displayed by John Rice Irwin is one built for a child and never used, perhaps because the child survived the immediate need for it. The coffin is at Irwin's Museum of Appalachia near Norris, Tenn. Coffin makers of the Smokies, including John McCaulley and Witt Shields of Cades Cove, liked the scarcer walnut boards, but worked with chestnut or pine when walnut wasn't available.

Photo from Jasper Morrow

The rush to cut and sell chestnut before the trees died of the blight resulted in this elaborate trestle and flume on Shuler Creek in 1918. Acid wood to be ground for its tannins, for the leather industry, rode the flume to the mouth of the creek at the Hiwassee River, where it was loaded into railroad cars

Index

V

Vananda, Lois, 44

W

Walker Cemetery, 124
Walker daughters, 17
Walker funeral, 18
Walker, John Beaver, 41
Walker, John Frank, 20
Walker, Nancy Caylor, 9-20
Walker sisters, 41, 137
Walker Valley, 9-20
Walker, W.C., 10
Walker's ox, 9
Walker's rifle, 12
walkingstick poplar, 73
Watson, Mamie, 88
Watson, Noah, 92
Waycaster, Luther, 38
Wears Valley, 39, 105
Webster, Herbert, 128
West Prong, 5
Whaley, Annie King, 46
Whaley, Burea, 101
Whaley, Crockett, 46
Whaley, L.C., Ruth and children,
   Harold, Everett, Frank, Arnold,
   Eugene, Helen, Nan, Charlotte, 101

Whaley, Marshall, 55
Whaley, Mary Brackin, 55
White Oak Flats, 6
White Shoe Co., 119
wild turkeys, 128
Wildcat Bluff, 82
Wildwood, 8
Wilkie, Elbert, 78, 117
Williams, Ben Mack, 66
Williams, Florence, 71
Williams, John Rooster, 65-72
Williams, Lena, 71
Williams, Maude, 68-72
Williamson, Wilma, 90, 124
Wilson Branch, 23
Wilson, Frank E., 67
Wilson, Jim, 92
Wonderland Hotel, 85, 96
wood hicks, 53
Woodruff, Luther, 92
Woodruff, Robert V., 90, 94
wooly adelgid, 134
wreck of No. 4, 51
wreck of No. 9, 50

Y

yellow poplar, 134